The Ghetto Blues. An Autobiography of Tammy Campbell Brooks' Trepidation, Tragedy, and Triumph

The Ghetto Blues

Copyright © 2018 by Tammy Campbell Brooks

All rights reserved. This book or any portion thereof

may not be reproduced or used in any manner whatsoever

without the express written permission of the publisher

except for the use of brief quotations in a book review.

Printed in the United States of America

First Printing, 2018

Graphic designer: **Dajsha Alejandro**
Cover designer: Myson and Tammy Campbell Brooks
Introduction: Tahirah Jessalyn Brooks

Author: Tammy Campbell Brooks
Title: The Ghetto Blues
Subject: Non-fiction/autobiography/memoirs
African American
Publishing 2018
Paradeyez Books Publishing
ISBN-13:
978-1732276802
Library of Congress Control Number: 2018942150

Acknowledgments

I would like to thank my sisters, Tina Campbell and Terrie Campbell Thornton, and my brother, James Edward Campbell Jr. for allowing me to tell not only my story but *our* story. It's not easy putting yourself and business out there for people to read and judge. I hope that I have done *our* family story justice.
I love you all to the moon and back.

I would like to thank the loves of my world, my husband, Emilio, my son, Bobby Jr. (Myson), and my daughter, Tahirah for accepting all of me and loving me wholeheartedly. We faced many challenges in our relationship dealing with my past. My husband and children's unconditional love is what keeps me going.

I would like to thank my aunt, Dorothy Nell Smith. My aunt set the foundation for my success. You are my role model. You worked hard to provide for your family, and you never made any excuses. Auntie instilled in me hard work and dedication. You told me that there's nothing better than having my own money; and you are correct.
Love and appreciate you for all that you have done for my family and me.

I dedicate this book to my parents, James Edward Campbell and Barbara Jean Campbell.
Dad accepted me as his own child, even though, he knew I'm not his biological daughter. He genuinely loved me the way he loved his biological children. My dad gave me his last name, my self-worth, and an identity with no questions asked.

Dad gave me confidence to strive and excel to be the best in school. He was my motivation to stay his "honor roll" student. Thank you, dad and I love and miss you.

To the strongest woman that I have ever met in my life; my best friend, my right-hand girl, my everything, my beloved mother taught me how to be a great mother, and how to overcome life's challenges. Mama instilled in me, strength, resilience, and to never give up no matter the circumstances. My mother will always be my #1 role model and warrior. I love you mama and I can't wait to get back to where we left off.

I hope you and daddy are proud of me and I have represented you well. You both were gone too soon but never forgotten. Rest in peace.

To my nieces, Argentina Campbell, Carla Marie Campbell Mitchell, Destiny Marie King, and Meoshia Nicole Campbell, I hope to inspire you to be strong women, but most importantly, strive to be great mothers, grandmothers, and so on. Be the change that you want to see in your children and lead by example. I know you ladies can do it. Auntie love you.

To my nephews, James Edward King, Carl Edward Campbell, and Anthony Campbell, may you be strong great men to lead for the next generations. Love you all.

To my brother- in- law, Richard Thornton, thank you for loving my baby sister unconditionally. I'm glad you chose each other. May your marriage continue to grow stronger each day. Love you.

To my great nieces and nephews, Kimora Baker, Deon Baker Jr, Faith Baker, Quentin Long, Samaya Estrada, Jaylen Allen, Ti'airrah Long, Mynell McMillion, Trillveon Mitchell, Kentrill Mitchell, Keon Mitchell, Kelonte Mitchell, and Quentavious Long. Auntie is setting the blueprint for you all to make better. I'm depending on you because you are the future generations. I Love you.

Special thanks to Dr. Raphael Ike, you played a huge part in my transformation into the woman I have become and strive to be better daily. God put you in my life for a reason. I'm proud of you and look forward to you telling your story. Congratulations on your success as a pharmacist. Much love and respect.

Special thanks to my good friend, Velma Garcia for telling me the things I need to hear rather than what I want to hear. I appreciate your uncut honesty. Thank you for reading excerpts of the book and giving your opinion. Love you, girl.

Special thanks to my childhood friend, Lynne Franklin who wrote, "Surviving The Impossible" for inspiring me to write a book after reading your life story. You are the quintessential example of a great mother and grandmother. I'm proud of you and so glad that we reconnected. Love you.

Special thanks to my childhood friend, Monica Anthony. You told me years ago that I need to write my story. Thank you for believing in me. Love you.

Special shout-out to all my cousins, Sharon Cline, Michael Burrel, James Burrel, Tracey Cline, Roselyn Bennett Lyons(late), Rochelle Bennett, Cedric Smith, Charles Cline, Evelyn Cline Brown, Kenneth Cline, Patricia Cline,

Kenneth Jones Sr., Tamara Cline, Kimberly Cline, Ronald Brown, and Ebony Brown.   Love you all.

To my uncles and their wives, Herbert Cline (Debra), Tommie Cline (Gwendolyn), and my mother's twin sister, my aunt, Ruth Ann Burrel (James (late) they are not twins but they look just alike. Dorothy's husband, Robert Smith. Love you.

To the late, Tom Cline and Emma Jane Cline, my grandparents. Thank you for my mother because without her, there would be no me. Rest in paradise.

To my late grandmother, Mamie Campbell, Aunt, Anna Brown, and Pauline Campbell (late). Love you.

Special shout-out to Dajsha Alejandro for designing my book cover. Much love and appreciation.

Special shout-out to my mother figure, Mary Dayson for your love and support through-out the years. Love you.

Special shout-out to my friend (my sister), Erica Bell and family (grandmother, mother, and sister, Nicole). I became part of the Bell family in my senior year of high school. Erica took me to get my driver's license. Love you, all.

Shout out to all my friends, the Emerson Bobcats and Fox Tech Buffaloes, Class of '87. We are going to heaven.

To all that I missed, my apologies.

Table of Contents

Library of Congress Control Number: 2018942150 2
Acknowledgments 3

Chapter 1 5
The Beginning of the Blues 5

Chapter 2 13
The Good Ole Blues 13

Chapter 3 20
Singing the Blues 20

Chapter 4 25
The Competitor in Me 25

Chapter 5 30
Survival by Any Means Necessary 30

Chapter 6 41
Pipe Dreams 41

Chapter 7 49
Lost in the Blues 49

Chapter 8 51
G.J.'s Blues 51

Chapter 9 79
The Lonely Blues 79

Chapter 10 101
The King of Blues 101

Chapter 11 108

King Don't Love NOBODY 108

Chapter 12 115
Goodbye Blue 115

Chapter 13 129
Myson 129

Chapter 14 143
How Do I Say Goodbye To What We Had? 143

Chapter 15 146
My Handmade 146

Chapter 16 159
The Never-Ending Blues 159

Chapter 17 163
Life after Death 163

Chapter 18 166
Crossed Paths 166

Chapter 19 174
The Transformation 174

Chapter 20 185
Ain't No Stopping Us Now 185

Chapter 21 193
Still I Rise 193

Chapter 22 197
Computer Love 197

Chapter 23 200
Let's Go Half On A Baby 200

Chapter 24 210
The Innocent One 210
Chapter 25 215
My New Love 215
Chapter 26 226
The End Is Near 226
Chapter 27 233
The Blue Ultimatum 233
Chapter 28 237
She Got My Nose 237
Chapter 29 243
Bells Will Be Ringing 243
Family Photos 257

Introduction

This book is about a young woman that experiences trepidation, tragedy, and triumph throughout her life stemming from childhood to an adult.

The purpose of this book is not only to entertain and to tell a story, but to help inspire young men and women to be resilient and to never give up because you are going through different challenges in your lifetime. Everyone goes through tough times in life, but it is a matter of being flexible (not easily broken) and being able to wipe your own tears and get back up.

In this book, you will go through different stages of emotions from tears, laughter, happiness, and joy to see a woman growing up in poverty and impoverished environments, but not letting the circumstances define her.

In *"The Ghetto Blues,"* men and women can relate to a lot of the experiences mentioned in the book, and we can all understand, and share a laughter at the same time.

This book is perfect for days that you feel like giving up and you need a reminder to keep on going.

The Ghetto Blues is more than an autobiography, it also sends a message. If we can inspire and change at least one person's life then that is one of our purposes accomplished. I have read my mom's book and it is the most amazing book I have ever read.

~ Tahirah J. Brooks

The Ghetto Blues is dedicated to my late parents,

Barbara Jean Campbell

And

James Edward Campbell Sr.

Rest in paradise.

I love you.

The Ghetto Blues

"Through my words, I will aspire to live forever."

~Tammy Campbell Brooks

Chapter 1

The Beginning of the Blues

𝄞

Growing up in a family with three siblings and my parents seemed normal, until I realized that something was very different about my siblings and me.

Mama, you got some explaining to do, "Why is my skin color so light?" A question I asked my mother, Barbara when I was seven years old. She always tried to ignore my logical question by responding with, "Ohhh, you and your sister, Terrie were left on the doorstep so I took both of you in and raised you." She often included my baby sister, Terrie who is three years younger than me in the conversation when I asked about *my* skin color.
My sister, Terrie is the same skin color as my older sister and brother, so Terrie's identity or skin color was not in question like mine.

I'm Tammy Campbell, the third oldest child born to Barbara Jean and James Edward Campbell Sr. I have an older sister, Tina, who is four years older than me. My brother, James Edward Jr. is two years older than me, and then it's me followed by my youngest sister, Terrie.

I grew up in The Eastside of San Antonio, Texas. We never owned a home growing up. We constantly leased and always moved. We never stayed in a residence for more than three years. Therefore, I was wise enough to know not to get acclimated to the environment or make friends because everything around me was temporary.

My favorite dog, Bobbie, who died of mange, was temporary. The kite that I flew on the baseball field that got tangled in a tree and eventually blew away was temporary. Sally, the little white girl in my kindergarten class with two blonde pigtails who moved to another classroom was temporary. Temporary like Texas weather. My parent's marriage of thirteen years was temporary, although it was the pain of their separating that left a permanent scar on everyone.

If I could give my dad an award for the best father, he would win hands down. He was a good dad. He loved all four of his kids. He was affectionate, caring, sensitive, and always gave us his undivided attention and time. He'd help my brother with his homework. He'd play basketball with my brother and cousin.

When my mother was at work, he would fix my baby sister's and my hair, and put our hair in his favorite hairstyle, one ponytail at the top of our heads. He never used the comb on our hair, only Royal Crown hair grease, the brush, and his hands.

He'd dig the grease out with the tip of his finger and rub the grease inside both hands and spread the grease all over our hair. He'd swoop the hair up with his hands and tie it with a rubber band. It always looked good to me because, my daddy did it. And daddy could do no wrong in our eyes.

My dad was a huge Dallas Cowboys fan, and I would sit on top of his lap and watch the games with him. He loved the cowboys, and so did my family.
We all gathered together to watch the football games outdoors on our black and white television set. We often watched T.V. outside as a family like some country folks.

The affectionate man that my dad was, we rarely, if ever got spankings. He has never ever hit any of us with a belt; instead, he'd spank us with the palm of his hand.

One time, when my dad spanked me with his hand, he cupped his hand so tight to lessen the pain of the hit or should I say, pat on the butt.

I pretended to cry like his extra cupped palmed hand hurt when he hit me.

"Aaaaawwwwwwwwww. I cried to make him feel bad for spanking me. He'd turn and grab me and say, "I'm sorryyyyy, babyyyy" as he hugged me tight. I'd let out another "Aawwwwwww" to make him feel more remorse so that he wouldn't ever do it again.
And he never did. My dad never wanted to hurt his kids, intentionally.

If there was an award for the best husband, my dad would come in last place.

My parents tied the knot when my mom was nineteen years old and pregnant with my oldest sister, Tina. My dad was twenty-one years old. Something tells me, it was a shotgun wedding. The reason being was, that I couldn't see a loving relationship between my parents.

I was eight years old when my dad was cheating with cataract-eyed, Rose. He messed around with all types of women during the marriage; white women, cataract-eyed women, *Bébé's* kids' women. I mean, you name it, my dad would claim it in the lost and found and put out a monetary reward if found. Yes, it was *that* serious.

I loved my dad because he was the only father that I've ever known.

𝄞 𝄞 𝄞

My mom was a strong woman that endured many heartaches in her life. She grew up in poverty in a home with two sisters and two brothers, and a father that often abused her mother.

My grandfather was like the man my mother married. The difference was, my mother, did not allow any man to lay a finger on her. Bobbie Jean didn't play.

My mother resembled the singer, Donna Summer and everyone called her, Bobbie Jean instead of Barbara.
I know it's a country name but the entire family except for the boys have 'country' names.
Bobbie Jean (my mother), and my aunts, Ruth Ann, and Dorothy Nell.

One day, I walked into my parent's bedroom and my heart dropped; it was the first time I experienced it and I couldn't fathom the sight of my mother crying.

"What's wrong, mama?" My eight-year-old voice spoke with concern. My mother turned to me and said,

"Pee Tee left me for another woman," with the saddest eyes filled with tears.

My dad's nickname was Pee Tee. We lived on F Street at the time of the separation, and our rent was $164.00 per month. My mother recently lost her job because she had a fight with cataract-eyed, Rose over my dad.

My dad was the supervisor at Crest Haven Nursing home, and my mom and Rose were nurses' aides.

My mother walked up to Rose to confront her about her husband, and the next thing you know, a fight between Rose and my mom was going down. I heard that my mom beat her ass and that was the reason she was fired. According to my mother, it was my dad's decision to fire my mom so that it would be easier for him to sneak around with Rose.

My dad eventually left his wife of thirteen years for cataract-eyed, Rose. It hurt being left for another woman, but it hurt more to see my mother cry. It was the first and last time I ever saw her cry.

It was a time when a little eight-year-old me became an eight-year-old little girl that worried about our livelihood along with my mother. I became a split image of her, a worry worm. I worried about the bills, food, and anything else my mother worried about. She had me to lean on and I had her. Although I couldn't do much about the situation, the fact of me being there by my mother's side was comforting.

𝄞 𝄞 𝄞

After my dad packed his things and moved in with Rose, my mom finally told me the truth about why my skin is so light. I sat curiously to listen to the words that cut like razor blades with alcohol poured on top of the wounds. "Pee Tee is not your daddy. Your daddy's name is Dewhight Dee Wilson." I started crying like the time when my favorite dog, Bobbie died.

My siblings asked me what's wrong. "Mama said that daddy is not my real daddy." I was devastated about what mama told me.

I ain't going to lie, hearing the man that I loved wasn't my real father was shocking and hurt deep into my soul. I resented and loved my mother all at the same time. I felt betrayed and more different than I'd already felt with my lighter skin complexion; I felt like, I was not a part of the Campbell family and didn't belong.

An outsider imposing my will on a family that had no choice but to accept me.

I never spoke about what my mother told me to my dad when we'd go visit him, but it was constantly on my mind.

I saw my dad as a stepdad but not my real dad. I loved him like a real dad and not like a stepdad. I don't care what the reality was, James Edward Campbell Sr. is my father. I don't care what the DNA says.

One sunny afternoon on Fargo Street, where my dad's mother lived, my sisters, my brother, and I was spending time with my dad. He was outside playing dominos along with some of the neighbors. My brother and I were playing in the front yard along with the next-door neighbor's kids and my cousin, Ronnie.

My brother, Edward was chasing me and I tried to get away from him, so I yelled, "Daddy, daddy, daddy" as I tried to escape him. I ran over to my daddy so that he could save me from my brother, and I will never forget my brother's hurtful words, "That's not your daddy. D.W is your daddy." I dropped my head with embarrassment because I didn't want my dad to know that I knew the *secret* of him not being my biological father. My dad told Edward to come here, grabbed his arm and told him, "I *am her daddy* and don't you ever let me hear you say that again."

At times, I don't know if it was best not knowing the truth, because the truth hurt like hell. My sisters and brother often teased me about Dewhight being my real father, and they nicknamed him, D.W. for DeWhight Wilson. The teasing from my siblings took a toll on me, and their words broke me like sticks and stones.

My mother told me the story of how she was going to leave me in the hospital when I was born, but her mother made her take me home. She kept the blanket over me so that my dad wouldn't see me. I could imagine my dad's face when he finally pulled back the blanket and saw a light, bright, and damn near white, Golden Child.

Surprise, daddy!

I must have stolen my daddy's heart right out of his chest because my dad came home drunk one night, when I was a newborn, and he told my mother, "Bobbie Jean, I know Tammy is not my daughter, but I love her just the same." My mother said that he never spoke another word about me or her infidelity.

I don't know how my dad accepted me without a fight, but I'm glad that he did. He didn't only accept me, I am *his* daughter. End of story.

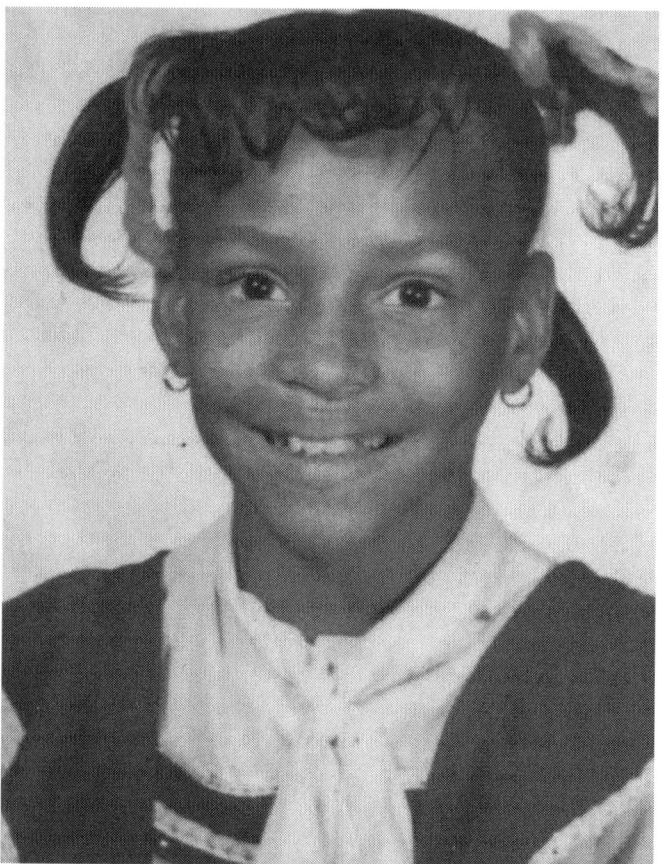
Tammy Age 9 (4th grade)

On the road again, I can't wait to get on the road again. Moving was a Campbell family's tradition as it seemed, because Pee Tee left Bobbie Jean with four hungry children and a crop in the field. My mother sang when Kenny Rogers, "Lucille" played on the radio.

Back to the ghetto of Sutton J. Homes on Panam Street we go. Mama didn't have a job and daddy was too busy with Rose and her kids, and no child support was coming our way. Daddy gave mama money for the rent, but she took the money and sold some of our best furniture— a dinette set, and our beloved microwave— to have enough money to move us back to the ghetto.

We lived in the same ghetto one year prior but moved to F Street because my dad never liked the projects.

During our previous short stay, we met the Taylor family. Ms. Bettie had about eight kids and she was one dark skinned, mean, ugly ass woman. Do you want to see evil? Ms. Bettie was Lucifer. She was short, pudgy, and black as night with jaundiced eyeballs. She looked like a black cat. She had kids the same age as my siblings and me, and we often played together.

Even though, Ms. Bettie was evil, at times, she gave us food when we had nothing to eat. She always kept a pantry full of food and kept it locked up. Her kids couldn't get food without her permission, and God forbid her kids get out of line, she would beat them black and blue with an extension cord. She didn't know what a belt was because I've never known her to use one. She always used an extension cord to 'discipline' her kids. Her oldest son, Alfred, became my mother's boyfriend.

Alfred is dark skinned, 6'1'' and weighed 225lbs, a solid build. The justice system unfairly incarcerated him for something dumb when he was younger.

𝄞 𝄞 𝄞

One night, my parents invited Alfred and Ms. Bettie to our home when we previously lived in Sutton homes, and during their visit, he unlatched one of the windows in our bedroom while no one was looking.

Later that night, my family and I went grocery shopping; we returned home and discovered that our television was G*O*N*E. My mother suspected that it was Alfred that stole our T.V.

Shortly after that incident is when we moved to F Street. Now, one year later, we were returning to the projects and Alfred is our new stepdad.

Alfred is eleven years younger than my mother. He visited us when we lived on F street, because he was my dad's friend. When my dad left, Alfred was there to keep my mother company.

Alfred didn't have children and he was twenty-two years old when he and my mom became a couple. My mother was thirty-three.

When my sister, brother, and I first learned that Alfred was dating our mom, we were not happy. In fact, we said all kinds of mean things about him, such as, "He ain't gone be my daddy. He's black and ugly."

We wanted no part of another man taking our beloved dad's place. Alfred had nothing to offer us and we didn't understand what my mother saw in him.

My mom had no job and four kids ranging from ages thirteen to as young as five to raise alone. Alfred promised that he would help raise us and he was true to his word.

During the time my mother was planning our move back to the Sutton Homes, there was another gentleman named, Larry that wanted to take my mom and her kids to California.

He was in the military, and we would tease my baby sister, Terrie and tell her that Larry was *her* daddy. Larry was also my father's friend. Who needs enemies with friends like Larry and Alfred willingly going behind my dad's back to get with his wife?

My mother turned Larry's invitation down and we moved back to Sutton Homes.

Chapter 2

The Good Ole Blues

"Eeeeewwwww, mama. Tina peed on us, again." My baby sister, Terrie and I would scream to my mom every time all three of us took baths together.

Tina was twelve or thirteen years old, and she had this strange fetish about peeing on my baby sister and me when we took baths together.

We often cried and exclaimed to my mother but I don't recall her doing anything about it. No matter how much we cried for Tina to stop, she just loved peeing on us, it made her happy.

One day, my sister, Terrie took a page out of Tina's handbook and took matters into her own hands. She waited until Tina got in the bathtub. Tina got in and she was washing herself getting her body all clean and fresh; her body full of bubble suds, as Terrie discretely stepped in the bathtub like our regular routine. And then, unexpectedly, Terrie spread her tiny bony legs wide open, and down came the bright golden shower sprayed all over Tina's body that was full of suds mixed with Terrie's pee.
TERRIE PEED ON TINA!
TERRIE PEED ON TINA!

We erupted with laughter and cheered. Tina was mad, but laughed along with us because it was funny how Terrie was so smooth about it.
TERRIE PEED ON TINA.

I want you to know that it was the most glorious and greatest days of our childhood to see the tables turned on my big sister.
It was like eating barbeque chicken and drinking grape soda for the first time. No, it was better than that, it was like beating the greatest athlete in the world at his own game. Taking the bully by the horn and beating him with his own horn.

What Terrie did to Tina that day stopped us from ever being peed on again.
TERRIE GOT TINA, GOOD.

Tina, Tammy, and Terrie were names that many admired because our names all begin with the letter "T."

People often got us mixed up, and would get confused about who was who, but not because we looked the same, but because our names were similar.

Alfred was one of the people that never got our names confused and he knew exactly who Tina, Tammy, and Terrie were.

Terrie and I were Alfred's favorite among my siblings because I was quiet, shy, and more observant and Terrie was the youngest. Tina and Edward weren't happy about him being with my mom, so I guess he sensed their disdain.

As a child, I was a reserved mama's girl. I followed my mother everywhere. When we visited my mother's side of the family, my sisters and brother played outside with my cousins, but me, I sat alongside my mother and listened to grown folk's conversations between my mother, her sisters, and my grandmother.

They would ask if I wanted to play outside with the other kids, but I often refused; and if I were to ever leave my mother's side, it wasn't for long periods of time, and she was always within my eyesight.
It was rare that I was seen without my mother.

𝄞 𝄞 𝄞

One day, my parents got into an argument, my mother jumped into the car to take off.

I was seven years old and I saw everything.

I opened the car door to our green four door Chevrolet and jumped in the backseat. She didn't have time to leave me or maybe she didn't mind me going with her, but she was trying to get away from my father as he hung on the car door trying to stop her. We got away from my father and sped off into the evening.

We stopped at a drugstore to get fruit, a hairbrush, a comb, and grease for my hair. If you know anything about my mother, she always kept her children's hair combed and clothes cleaned.

We checked into a decent hotel room that consisted of two beds, a queen size and a twin bed. The queen bed was located straight ahead when you entered the room, while the twin bed sat to the right of the front door. The room was nice and had a big antique mirror that hung over the queen size bed. It had a television toward the center left and lamps that sat on the nightstands of each bed.

Even though, it had two separate beds, I knew my mother didn't expect me to sleep in the twin bed *alone*. I have three siblings and I have never slept in a bed alone, and I was not accustomed to doing so and felt that I shouldn't sleep *alone* this night, either.

We ate our fruit and watched television and then we went to sleep. I slept right next to my mother and watched the empty twin bed fade into darkness as I drifted off into a deep slumber.

We awakened the next day. My mother combed my hair, and we returned home to my dad.

I will never forget the tranquility of that hotel room; it was quiet, peaceful, and I didn't want to leave.

𝄞 𝄞 𝄞

The separation took its toll on my parents, and we kids suffered immensely, too.

We were like a revolving door; visiting my dad, his new woman, and her kids. And then going home to my mother and her new man.

My dad's relationship with Rose didn't last long at all, like I suspected it wouldn't. My dad left a good woman, and there would never be anything of honor or good fortune coming his way.

Rose cheated on him with the father of one of her kids. My dad left and started another relationship with another woman that had three kids by three different men. His new woman was Della.

Della is mixed with a little bit of Mexican, but not enough mixture to consider her biracial. I would say that she is 25% Mexican and 75% Black American.

She was short and pudgy with thick black hair.
She had a daughter named, Betty Sue, a son, Quincy, and the youngest daughter, Tyeshia.

It wasn't too long after Rose, and my father called it quits that he and Della became a couple.

My father and Della were dating for a year or so when my dad put a little birdie in my ear for me to tell my mother that he was ready to come back home and be a husband.

I was so excited and couldn't wait until my dad took us home so I could give my mother his message. I was ready to be a family, again.

I was tired of going between families and I was not happy seeing Alfred or my dad's different women in our life. As any child wants, they want to see their parents together. I knew my mom would feel the same way when I tell her what daddy said. But she didn't, she immediately shot my dreams of becoming a family down. My mother's response hurt me as much as the day I saw her crying in her room when my dad left her for Rose. Well, not quite as hurtful, but it was close because I wanted my family back together.

"He had done too much and it would never be the same," was my mom's response to my dad and her reconciling. My mother didn't bat an eye nor hesitate, and she didn't think twice of a reconciliation with my dad.

James Campbell took a fine time to leave Bobbie Jean with her four hungry children and a crop in the field. My beloved father had messed up for the last and final time.

My mother let it be known— make no mistake about it— that the marriage was over, and she didn't look back.

She took her four hungry children and a crop in the field and decided to grow corn out of that crop. She took no meal and made it into oatmeal. A no-ball was made into a snowball. My mother took her weakness and vulnerability for my dad and became a strong SHERO in my eyes. She was indeed my Shero from that day forward. It was a subconscious Shero at the time, because I was too young to understand, but on that day, my dear mother imprinted a blueprint of a strong black woman that would forever be etched into my legacy.

My mother was a GODDESS of strength with a backbone that rejected my beloved father despite our hardship.

My mom closed her marriage chapter, but I wish I could say it was for the best.
She didn't want cheating daddy back. Nooooo way.

We resided in the same apartment as the last time we lived in Sutton Homes. My mother went to the office and talked to the manager and requested the same apartment.

2904 N. Panam Street was located on the outskirts of the projects. The families that lived alongside Panam Street in the brown colored apartments were the 'classy' families, and these families lived in the projects not by choice, but due to poverty.

In other words, the projects were the last place we wanted to live. Clifford, and my brother's best friend, Charles, and the Pettis family all lived on the outskirts of Sutton Homes in the brown apartments, and they fit the description of a 'classy' family like the Campbells.

Anyone that lived in the white apartments of Sutton Homes were considered the ghetto people of the projects.

There was this family that lived in the white apartments in Sutton Homes, and this family was feared by many that lived in the ghetto. I will call them, the Dukes in order not to disclose their real identity. The Dukes were a huge family of terrorizers. Ms. Dukes had about twelve kids, and they ranged in age from adults to elementary school ages. The older daughters, in their twenties, thought they were the baddest bitches that ever walked this planet. They were known to carry switchblades and they didn't hesitate to use them. When you fought one, then you better be prepared to fight the rest.

They once jumped my friend's mother when she was at a nightclub, and from that day forward, her mother feared them.

The Dukes' girls fought any gender, any age group, any animal of the animal kingdom, it didn't matter; they were GANGSTER. The younger kids were bad as hell but everyone knew not to mess with the Dukes' kids or family. This was a no-no.

My family heard all the tales of the Dukes but didn't take heed; we played with the girls the same age as we were. We played with them quite frequently so it wasn't a big deal until my sister, Terrie got into it with one of the Duke's girls that was the same age as her.

Terrie was nine years old, but her getting into it with another nine-year-old, shouldn't have been a big deal, so I thought. My sister and the little girl had an altercation that escalated like an inferno out of control.

My mother like the Dukes' family didn't play when it came to her kids. I could never forget the vision of this wild, wild, west scene that was only seen in Hollywood movies.

It was a nightmare, but our reality.

Alfred and I were in our home in the hallway, on our knees, dodging the gunfire between the Dukes and my mother.

Alfred was in the hallway crying and shaking, but my mother stood at the backdoor loading and reloading her 38 Smith and Wesson pistol firing back at the Dukes family.

I was twelve years old, and all I could think of was: why was Alfred on this floor when he should be helping my mother fire back at them son of a bitches?

I was not scared, and even though, I was told to stay down, it took everything in me to restrain myself because I wanted to help my mom. When I'm angry, I fold and bite my tongue under my teeth. When you see that in me, you better run because that means I'm super mad.

My tongue was folded, and I was like a snake ready to attack. I wanted a piece of them Dukes bad— so bad that it hurt.

NOBODY messes with my mama!

Pop, Pop, Bam, Bam continued for at least ten minutes or maybe longer or shorter, I didn't keep the time. When you thought it was over, there was more gunfire, but not from the Dukes. The bullets were coming from Bobbie Jean!

My mother was a bad mother shut yo mouth. I watched her the entire time as if I was her shield. It was a mental shield, but nonetheless, I was her invisible protector. She had no fear; and that very night with the gunfight between the Dukes family, she sent a message to the Dukes and the entire community of Sutton J. Homes, and the message was loud and clear; do not fuck with the Campbells family.

The Dukes were an army, but my mother was a one-woman soldier, a fearless warrior, a SHERO. I knew this about my mother, but the Dukes didn't know, but after that night, they learned.

The Dukes! The Dukes! My mother, my shero went pound for pound and round for round with the Dukes family.

The toughest family in the projects; but they met their match and maybe a match that was well overdue.

The strangest part about the night was that after all the gunfire subsided, the serene sound of the night returned. It was like the world stopped moving and you couldn't hear or see the darkness.
No sirens.
No ambulance.
No police.
No arrest.
No fatalities.
No evidence.
Like it never happened.

Chapter 3

Singing the Blues

I used to go to parties

And stand around
'Cause I was too nervous
To really get down

The music of the legendary Marvin Gaye, "Got To Give It Up" blasting through the speakers in 1977.
My parents loved to throw house parties back in the days. They had some bomb parties when we lived on F Street.
The home came with a built-in bar and a big backyard along with big bedrooms that my sisters, brother, and I had to stay in whenever they threw a house party.
But because the rooms were roomy didn't mean that we stayed inside them the entire time.
No, we were disobedient and wanted to see, "What's going on."
We made several trips to the bathroom and kitchen to spy on our parents and their guests.
There was plenty of alcohol, dancing, bell-bottoms pants with silk vests worn by the men. They had big afros and fly patent leather shoes. The women wore dresses, wigs, and some had natural afros like the men.
My dad resembled Marvin Gaye with the exception that he was a little under 5'8. Marvin was over 6'0 feet, but my father wore the same beard and their skin complexion was almost identical.
In fact, my dad sung in a band, and he sang many of Marvin's tunes; he played the piano and was good.

He often played, 'Colour My World' by Chicago on the facility's piano when we visited him at work at Crest Haven Nursing home. My dad was musically gifted and talented.

The Campbells family ate, slept, and breathed Rhythm & Blues, and good music in general despite the genre.

My parents frequented the record store located on Hackberry Street almost weekly to buy a vinyl 33-inch or 45-inch record.

They bought music from artists and groups, such as, Marvin Gaye, Earth Wind and Fire, The Real McCoy, Ike and Tina Turner, The Temptations, KC & The Sunshine Band, The Stylistics, The Spinners, The Isley Brother, The Emotions, The Bee Gees, Chicago, Frankie Beverly & Maze, Kool & The Gang, The O'Jays, and The Commodores.

I think you get my drift on how much music played in our life; the lists of different music artists go on and on. We could have owned a record store, that's how much music my parents purchased.

During the summer when my parents would go to work and my siblings and I were on summer break and left alone, we would play the record player like there was no tomorrow, and the living room was our dance floor.

"Do The Hustle" was one of our favorite songs. We would line up and do exactly what the music told us to do, "Do the Hustle."

We were never shy about shaking what our mama gave us, and until this day, if the music plays, we will groove to it until the break of dawn and be ready to continue the next day.

The Campbell family's love, happiness, and sometimes sadness revolved around music and it got us through the good and bad times.

It was mostly happiness and love when it came to Rhythm & Blues music.

My mother had a friend named Julia and she worked with my mom and dad at Crest Haven Nursing Home. She often came to my parents' house parties.

Julia had three daughters and one of the daughters' named, Tangy has huge breasts and she was my brother's age.

The daughters had to stay inside the room along with us while their mother partied with our parents. My brother, Edward loved Tangy and those big titties. He would cop him a feel more often than anyone knew. Tangy didn't seem to mind; in fact, she relished him, grabbing her titties because she kept coming back for more.

My mom thought Tangy's mother, Julia came to our house often because she wanted an affair with my dad, but it wasn't my dad that Julia was interested in, it was *my mom* that caught her eye. Julia was a lesbian with three kids, and shortly after Julia let her intentions known for my mom, we never saw her or her daughters again.

𝄞 𝄞 𝄞

We were some bad kids, so my brother copping a feel on Tangy big titties was many things that we did growing up.

My parents left us in the car often when they went to Globes shopping center, and it was because we were bad.

When they left us in the car, my brother, the ringleader, would see other Mexican kids left in the car, and we would pick fights with them.

Back in those days, kids were left in the car all the time without fear of someone kidnapping them. My brother would roll down the car window and curse out the little Mexican kids. Before you know it, we were all in the car throwing the Mexican kids the birdie finger, sticking out our tongues, and cursing them in Spanish.

We would say, "F*ck yo mama," in Spanish, over and over, and "b*tch." I have no idea how we learned those Spanish curse words, but we knew them well.

The Mexican kids would curse us back in Spanish, but we never knew what they were saying and neither did we care.

We were bored, and our parents told us not to get out of the car before they went into the shopping center.

My parents took longer than expected, and we would tell each other to go see what they were doing. We'd talk one of us to go in and check on our parents. None of us wanted to go because we were already *warned* not to get out the car. Sure enough, the one that got out the car was going to get a butt whipping from *mama*. Mama, unlike daddy, whipped our butt with no regrets or remorse. There was never no, "I'm sooooorrry, babbby," like my dad. Nope, when mama whipped our butt, she meant business and if we did it again, we were going to get another one.

When we would act up in public, my mother would say, "You are going to get a whipping when we get home." As soon as we got home, we'd run straight to the room to put on extra clothing to lessen the pain of her belt. But 90% of the time, mama would forget all about the whipping by the time we got home. We still put on extra clothing in case she remembered.

The thing was, to act bad at the beginning of the trips, instead of towards the end when we were almost home because you were guaranteed to get a butt whipping.

We stayed in the car a lot while my parents shopped; the only time we would go inside is when we were getting new shoes. We had to get out to make sure the shoes fit our feet. And when one of us got new shoes, we ALL got new shoes.

My mother made a lot of our clothes, too. She had a sewing machine and would go to Fabric Warehouse on E.Houston Street to get sewing material to make us dresses. She and my aunt, Ruth Ann loved to sew.

My mother dressed my baby sister and I like twins. She'd comb our hair in the same hairstyle, too. I guess mama secretly wanted twins, but she never had any, so Terrie and I were her *bootleg* copy version of twins.

When mama pressed our hair, we would ask her, whose hair was the longest? Our hair stayed close in length, the only difference was Terrie's hair was thicker than mine.

My mother washed our hair with Zest soap, because we had no shampoo or conditioner.

The same Zest soap that would burn our "goochie nows." That's what mama told us to call our private parts, "goochie nows." When we'd wash our goochie nows with that Zest soap, it would burn like hell. I never knew what kind of ingredients the makers of Zest put into the soap back in the days, because it burned like lye.

The Zest soap made our hair nappier. When we'd ask mama about whose hair was the longest, she could never say, but she would say that Terrie's hair was nappier, but her hair took a lot less heat to straighten, and my hair was nappy, but it took more heat than Terrie's to get it straight. She could run the straighten comb through Terrie's hair twice to get it straight, but mine took a lot more.

23

Terrie had a shine to her hair, but I had the sandy reddish hair that never shined.
    My mother took good care of our hair and kept it combed, every day.
She took good care of her kids and *always* put us first.

Left to right (Dad, Terrie, Mom, Alfred, Edward, Tina, and Tammy) Pic taken in 1980.

Chapter 4

The Competitor in Me

After the gunfire exchange between the Dukes and mama, we never had an issue with them or anyone else. It was a silent hood creed respect; nonetheless, it was still respect, and knowing where the Dukes and Campbells family tolerance level stood. We didn't fuck with them and they didn't fuck with us. Excuse my language.

As strange as it may seem, I think it drew us closer to the Dukes. We remained friends with the younger Dukes' girls, Valerie and Shay, and neither of us brought up the incident; it was business as usual in the ghetto.

Valerie, Shay, my sister, Terrie and I often danced together along with my brother's best friends' brother, Craig.

Craig was cool. He is five years older than me and he choreographed a dance routine for my sister, the Dukes girls, and me to perform. The song choice was, "Firecracker" by Mass Production. He would put us in line (Terrie, Valerie, Shay, and me) according to who danced the best or should I say, who did his choreography the best.

It was always between Valerie and me that would get the number one spot to be first in line as the best dancer.

He switched Valerie and me almost every day when we came to rehearse. I was very competitive. If she out danced me and he moved her ahead of me, I would start dancing even harder. I would work and thrust my tiny small frame booty around. I couldn't take being second or someone out dancing me. It was unfathomable. I was a competitor, especially, when it involved the art of dancing. The Rhythm & Blues were instilled in me and inherited from Pee Tee and Bobbie Jean's obsession of great music. There was no way I would let anyone out dance me.

Finally, I was moved back to the spot I rightfully deserved; first place as the best dancer as I tore that dance routine up like a government cheese sandwich. I was getting it like the song said, a "firecracker" that couldn't stop popping.

🎼 🎼 🎼

Competitiveness was natural and came automatic to me. I was so competitive that I'd competed with myself in my sleep.
When the cockroaches that lived in the same house tried to run me out of my own bed, I had to show those critters who was boss.

One night, I was tired of those roaches crawling all over me while I tried to sleep; I'd gone into the kitchen and got a big butcher's knife and placed it beside my bed.
My mother came into my room and saw the knife next to me and asked what I was doing with it.
"It's for those roaches. I'm tired of them. I'm going to stab them "cocker roaches." I was irritated with those roaches crawling on me.
I pronounced it, "cocker roaches" not cockroaches.
"Guuuurlllll, you're crazy."
My mother emphasized "gurl" while laughing.
She thought it was funny.
The next day, I was the talk of the family about pulling a knife on cockroaches. My mother called her mother and her sisters to tell them about how I slept with a butcher's knife next to me to kill roaches.
I heard her on the phone yapping, laughing, and telling all my business on how dead serious I was on stabbing roaches.
It didn't occur to me the humor nor did I understand the dynamic of using a 'butcher's knife' to kill roaches as opposed to a shoe or roach spray. I didn't get it.
The only thing I understood at that time was, they were getting on my nerves and competing for my bed. It was nothing funny about eating, sleeping, and living with roaches, and I had to get rid of them by any means necessary.
Project roaches gave me a lifetime of blues and so did my competitive nature.
I still hate roaches to this day.

🎼 🎼 🎼

My competitiveness didn't end with dancing and winning against the roaches.

I was in fifth grade and my teacher's name was Mrs. Hastings. I was a straight "A" student. I have never received a "B" ever in my life on my report card since attending elementary school, and I planned to keep it that way. My dad called me his straight "A" student. I was proud when he called me his honor roll student and how he bragged about my grades.
I took great pride in my grades, especially, my spelling grades.
Throughout fifth grade, I received all 100's on each spelling quiz.

One day, my class was about to take our spelling test. I knew I had to go to the restroom and I should have asked Mrs. Hastings prior to the start of the quiz if I could go. "I could wait" my head said, but my ten-year-old body disagreed.
My nerves along with the intensity of making sure I spelled each word correctly and not ruin my perfect 100% spelling score got the best of me; my urge to use the restroom grew stronger and stronger as Mrs. Hastings called out each word. It intensified like a volcano about to erupt. It felt like my body went into a paralyzed anaphylaxis state of shock. I no longer had control of holding it in; and without another moment of hesitation, the warmth of bodily fluids ran down my legs, and inside my friend Kelly's shiny brown leather boots that she let me wear that day.
 Pee ran onto the classroom floor next to Erick's desk who sat in the desk in front of me.
My friend, Kelly and I exchanged shoes quite often because I loved her boots. She was a sweetheart and I'm not sure if she liked my shoes or not, but she wanted to please me so she would let me wear her boots whenever I saw her wear them to school. I had her boots on this day. I loved boots and hats.
When my mother and I would go to the Goodwill, I'd put all kinds of hats on my head and say, "Look at me mama" to get her opinion on how they made me look.
My mama would shake her head side to side meaning, I was something else.

The spelling quiz ends and Erick bends over to reach inside his desk for his book so we can begin the next lesson. I watched him because I knew he would see my pee and say something. It didn't take long. I watched him as he said *real loud*,

"Ooooooooooooh, somebody done, Unt, Unt, I ain't gone say nothing," Erick shook his head side to side and turned back around in his desk.

He was a class clown and the reason he sat in front of me and not in his *original* seat. He was supposed to be sitting in a row at the back of the class since his last name begins with the letter "Y."
Our assigned seats were prioritized in alphabetical order according to our last names. Mrs. Hastings moved Erick in front of me to be closer to her, to keep an eye on him and try to control some of his behavior.

Mrs. Hastings stood up from her desk to see what Erick was talking about and she looked directly at me,
"Tammy, did you do *that*?"
She didn't call it pee or urine. She called it, "that."
I wanted to say, "What is **that** you're talking about?" But I didn't because I knew exactly what she meant by *that*.

I was red as an apple and most certainly embarrassed in front of all my classmates and my crush, Michael. I nod my head facing downward meaning, "Yes." I couldn't verbally answer because I couldn't look up and face all those fifth graders staring at me.

No one laughed because our class was accustomed to classmates peeing on themselves. My friend, Bettie, Peanut, and even my crush all had accidents in Mrs. Hastings' fifth grade class. We were known as the *pee-pee* class.

Mrs. Hastings told me to go to the restroom. I never understood why teachers told students to go to the restroom 'after' they already gone to the restroom on themselves. I thought to myself, "Mrs. Hastings, didn't you see me go to the restroom? Don't you see the evidence, I don't need to go, again."

Instead of going to the restroom, I went to the nurse's office to call my mother.

I returned to the classroom and tried to return those wet brown leather boots to my friend, Kelly, but she didn't want them and told me that I could take them home. I didn't want the boots either; my dry clean shoes that she had on her feet look more appealing after all, than her soggy wet boots. I wanted my dry shoes back, but she wasn't going for it.

The only good thing about that day was, I went home early and I kept my 100% spelling streak record alive.
 I didn't want a score of 95 or 90. Oh no, that would never do. I wanted a perfect spelling score of 100.
And guess what?
My pissy competitive ass got my 100.
YES!

Chapter 5

Survival by Any Means Necessary

I can go on for days telling stories of how competitive I was in school and life in general.

I played many sports during middle school, but my best sport was cheerleading. I loved cheerleading because it is a form of dance.

I started cheering when I began sixth grade, I was in the pep squad. We were so poor that my mother sewed my pep squad uniform by hand with a needle and thread.

She would design and make our clothes with her sewing machine when my parents were together, but since the separation, we lacked many material things and necessities.

My mom went from the frying pan into the fire in her relationship with Alfred. They argued day and night, night and day. I would go inside the closet and cover my ears to shield the noise of their arguments. I never knew what they argued about, but it was constant and I wished I was exaggerating. I wanted Alfred gone. There were no physical fights, but a whole lot of unnecessary arguments.

One day, the phone company accidentally turned our telephone on. And I was calling random numbers, and I dialed 411 and talked to an operator. It was a gentleman that knew my mother.

I couldn't believe my ears, and I don't know how we got on the topic of my mother. I wanted a better man for her so maybe I tried to hook her up? I talked with him and I hung up the phone and ran to ask my mother about him. He told me his name, J.D., and how he knew my mother, so when I told her who he was, she knew him and knew that he worked for the phone company.

I had to get J.D. back on the phone, immediately. He had a decent job and he would probably be better for my mother than Alfred.

I began dialing 411 for about an hour or so, I must have ran that phone bill up even more dialing 411 and hanging up on every operator that wasn't him.

Unfortunately, I never got him back on the phone and the hook up between J.D. and my mother was doomed.

Alfred it is, no matter how I tried to get rid of him.

Alfred wasn't a horrible person; he was a damaged *young* man. His entire family suffered from the abuse of his evil mother, Ms. Bettie. His sisters and brothers were damaged, too.

Damaged parents damage their kids through abuse, neglect, or abandonment, and it was passed down from generation to generation. It was the typical life story of many Black Americans in the ghetto.

Alfred did his best to take care of us, and the little bit of money that he had, he gave to my mother.

He was a provider, but with no education and in his twenties, he still had a lot to learn; and at times, his immaturity showed.

After the incident between cataract-eyed, Rose and my mother, my mom never worked. She was a stay home mom and we depended solely on Alfred's income. His job was unloading trucks at the truck stop and he was paid cash daily. He would spend all day at the truck stop and brought home twenty, thirty and sometimes fifty dollars if he was *lucky*. He gave it all to my mother for food. Some days there were no trucks to unload because there was a lot of competition from other black men trying to feed their families.

A lot of times Alfred brought nothing home.

At the Truck Stop, the company would throw away huge packages of meat, such as, briskets, ribs, steaks, pork roasts, and Alfred would go inside the dumpster and get the meat.

We would call my mother's family to buy the meat from us for five or ten dollars a pack. We kept some meats for ourselves, but most of the time, we sold them for money to pay the bills.

The welfare system was a joke when it came to receiving benefits for poor black families.

The social workers would come to our home unexpectedly to see if a man was living in the home. If there was a man caught in the household, the benefits were cut immediately.

There were times when we left Alfred's clothes in an area where they could be conveniently hid in case the social worker came by unannounced.

During the separation, my parents concatenated this lie that my dad gave my mom $200 a month for child support, because if she didn't have any income, we couldn't receive food stamps or public housing.

My dad had to write a letter every six months for us to continue receiving food stamps; and at times, he didn't want to write the letter. My mom had to beg him for the letter when it was time to renew our food stamps.

My dad paid my mom back for not taking him back and for being with Alfred, and it was the reason he gave mama such a hard time writing the letters. But what my dad failed to realize was, he wasn't only hurting mama, he was hurting his children, too.

I never knew why we didn't write the letters ourselves, instead of begging daddy.

𝄞 𝄞 𝄞

After my parent's separation, we never received a dime from my dad. Sometimes, he would buy hotdog buns and wieners to take home with us after we visited him. But we often went to bed hungry.

My mom never filed for child support against him. She never wanted the court system in our family's affairs.

We would go without food a lot, it was so bad that Alfred would wait until McDonalds on Walters street closed for the night and whatever food they threw away, he would jump inside the dumpster and get it out and bring it home for us to eat.

The fries and hamburgers would be warm and delicious. We didn't care about maggots or other bugs that could have been in the food; we were hungry and we didn't care where the food came from, we were happy to have something to eat.

The school meals were our last meals of the day if Alfred didn't unload a truck.

We were so hungry one day that my baby sister was throwing up. My sister being sick from hunger, devastated my mother and broke her heart.

𝄞 𝄞 𝄞

One day, it was freezing cold outside, temperatures had to be in the low 20's because there was ice on the ground.

My mother had a food stamp appointment. She didn't have bus fare to catch the bus so she decided to walk from the Sutton Homes to the food stamp office located on Cherry Street. It was about a fifteen-minute drive in a car.

I wanted to go with her because there was no way I would let my mother walk alone in that weather. I've always been afraid that something bad would happen to my mom and the reason I stayed by her side. I couldn't bear my life without my precious mother.

I was eleven years old, and I was freezing. We had only one pair of gloves that belonged to my mother, and my hands were numb. I didn't complain because I was trying to be strong, and besides, I knew that my mom would take off her gloves and put them on my hands, and *she* would suffer the pain of cold hands. I didn't want my mother's hands cold. She kept asking about my hands and if I was cold, but I denied it until I couldn't take it anymore; we were passed New Braunfels Street when I admitted that my hands were cold. My mom took her gloves off and gave them to me. I held her hand in mine one by one alternating on each side to keep her hands warm as we continued to walk to get our food stamps.

It was a long, devastating walk, but my mom walked with not ONE complaint and endured it all; she knew her kids needed safe sanitary food and not food from McDonald's dumpster.

𝄞 𝄞 𝄞

Alfred got a job at Woodlake Country Club located on FM78. He was the dishwasher and would bring home leftover food from his job. When he got the dishwasher job, we never had to eat out of McDonald's dumpster, again.

He brought home all kinds of food and desserts, along with his paycheck. He gave it all to mama, every penny of it.

She gave him some spending cash for his pockets, but all the money went into the household for food and bills.

While hunger became the least of our worries since Alfred got the job at Woodlake Country Club, we were still poor.

My love for cheerleading let me know how poor we were when my mother made my pep squad uniform by hand.

My love for cheer never swayed. I tried out for the cheerleading squad the next school year, seventh grade.

🎼 🎼 🎼

We had tryouts inside the Emerson's girl's gymnasium. All my close friends were trying out since we all were in the pep squad together. We spent many days after school practicing and getting ready for the *main event* to make the cheer squad.

My friend, Lottie and Buffy who grew up with me in the Sutton Homes. My friends, Tonya, Antionette, and Monica were there and some of them were among the participants. The instructions were to choose two cheers, one cheer had to be a Skills cheer and the other cheer, do whatever cheer you want. Both cheers had to include at least two different jumps.

When it was my time to tryout, there were four judges that sat at a long table writing and critiquing each of the participants.

If there was one area I was confident in, it was dance and cheer.

I did my Skills cheer first. The Skills cheer was technical with hands, legs, and movements on point.

Hands and head straight, movements to perfection.
My second cheer was one of my favorite cheers, and I had it down to the "T" like the first initial, "T" in my name. The cheer was called, "Boogie."

Boogie is the name we say
And Boogie is the game we play
So Boogie, put your feet on the ground
Boogie, just get on down
Boogie, put your feet on the ground
Boogie, just get on down
Now, BOOGIE!

When performing the Boogie cheer, I added all kinds of extra moves that were not originally part of the cheer. The extras that I added were the bomb diggidy. Especially, how I ended the cheer and the movement I did to wrap it up. I orchestrated it like no other participant.

There were many participants doing the Boogie cheer, but none of them could do Boogie close to how I did Boogie. But of course, I knew it and the reason I chose the cheer. I out strategized my cheer competition. I knew who could cheer and I knew strengths and weaknesses.

All participants were done and it was time for the results. There could only be *five Cheerleaders* so many girls were going to be disappointed and must continue being in the pep squad.

I didn't want to be in pep squad, I wanted to be on the field leading the cheers and cheering for the crowd and football team.

In Pep squad, no one hardly recognized you because there were so many of us that we all looked and sounded the same when chanting cheers. Pep squad was for mediocrity cheerleaders and sixth graders entering middle school.

I wanted to be a REAL Cheerleader.

The names were being announced, I was confident and nervous all at the same time. I knew they had a spot for me because after my Boogie cheer, I got so many praises from the girls that confirmed I tore it up.

The results were in……and names were called, "The first Bobcat cheerleader is……
Stephanie W.!" The lady announced with enthusiasm.
The girls clapped for Stephanie being the first cheerleader.
"The next Bobcats cheerleader is……
Stephanie Wr.!"
More congratulatory applause from the girls.
"And the next Bobcat Cheerleader is……
Dannette K.!"
There were only two spots left and I was not happy that my name wasn't called. The confidence that I had after completing my Boogie cheer was tested at an all-time high at that moment. *I was nervous.*

The lady continued to announce the FINAL two cheerleaders.

"The Co-Captain of the Emerson Bobcats is....... Tonya D.!"
The girls applauded even louder. Tonya was a sweetheart and she was not only a great cheerleader; she was gifted in band and very smart. She was a straight "A" student and now, the Co-Captain of the cheerleaders.

What is going on? I thought to myself. I knew I was the best cheerleader, but my name wasn't called and everyone was congratulating the girls that made it.

I couldn't hear or feel much of anything because my confidence was shot and my heart beat out of my chest. Between the noise and the jumping up and down from the cheerleaders that made it, I couldn't hear nor comprehend why my name wasn't called. I wanted to cry, but then I heard the **final announcement**.......

"And the **Captain** of the Cheerleaders is......(drum roll) TAMMY CAMPBELL!"
Everybody went wild! My friends were like "Tammy, you made *Captain* of the Cheerleaders!"
ME? Little ole, Tammy Campbell from the ghetto made CAPTAIN of the cheerleaders.

I still get goose bumps thinking of the day when I made the Captain of Cheerleaders at Emerson Middle School.

We were announced by the lowest to the highest scores.
I couldn't, but then again, I could believe that I made Captain of the cheerleaders.
They saved the best for last and scared me in the process.

I knew I was bad and if anyone deserved a spot on the Bobcats cheer squad, it was me, Tammy Campbell.
When it came to cheering on that field for the football team, I didn't hold anything back.

I would pop-lock, moonwalk, you name it, I did all the latest dances. I was not only a cheerleader; I was an entertainer, like the king of pop, Michael Jackson.

I don't want to toot my own horn, but I was pretty special out there and I kept the crowd entertained. I gave them their money's worth.

All fifty cents to a dollar's worth. The cost of admission into the football games in those days.

I was a shy little girl, but when it came to dance and cheer, I didn't hold back.

A friend's mother made my cheer uniform.

My mother couldn't make this uniform by hand, it would be too embarrassing being the captain of the cheerleaders with a needle and thread sewn uniform sewed by my mother's hands. We didn't have much money, but we were able to pay for my uniform, pom-poms, and shoes.

I put 100% into everything that I've ever done. I was a self-motivator and I didn't consider myself 'smart.' I was a hard worker and I put forth full effort.

A competitor. And the fear of failure was my motivator.

Going to bed without food was my motivation.

Eating out of the McDonald's dumpster motivated fear.

The unsafe and crime driven environment in the ghetto was my greatest motivation. I *hated* my living arrangement and being born into poverty.

I put all that motivation into my school work and sports. I escaped my reality through school and sports. I found comfort in being the best. I was the best cheerleader. I was the best dancer. I was the best soccer player. I was the best track hurdler until I fell during a track meet.

The fall tore and scarred my knees for life. I won first place at all the track meets in the hurdles; there was no one that was a greater athlete than me when I ran the hurdles. I perfected the hurdles so well because the cheer jump, the herkey was my favorite jump.

The herkey cheer jump was the same form that I used to jump the hurdles. I did the herkey jump all the time when cheering so I carried the same technique and applied it towards my track skills.

On your mark, get ready, said, goooo…. (The sound of the starter gun rang in the air)
I took off with enough speed to jump the first hurdle.
I jumped the second hurdle…
And then, it happened, the click clack as my friend, Monica described the sound of the hurdle as it along with me hit the ground.

I didn't look at my knees, I saw the hurdlers running ahead of me. Everything was surreal and in slow motion.
I must have had an adrenaline rush because I felt no pain, only the disappointment that the best hurdler was down on the ground for the *first* time.

I got up off the track made of red gravel and jumped the remaining hurdles to regain my number one place.
I beat every girl in my race even after falling and failing behind. I don't know how I did it. It was the competitor in me.

When my track time was compared to the other girls that ran in different heats, I placed fourth!
I couldn't believe it. I was hot. I placed fourth in the hurdles. I didn't receive a ribbon because first through third are the only ribbons awarded. I only cared about first place; any other placement was a loss according to my standards.
I was the best and that meant, first place or no place.

My coach came to me after I finished the hurdles to evaluate my injuries, and my knees were scared with blood running down. My knees were bruised bad.

I still had the 400-meter dash to run and my coach wanted to pull me and have someone else take my place. I didn't want anyone to take my place. I wanted to finish what I started.

The trainer wrapped both of my knees with a white bandage and I got back out there.
I felt the pain in my knees, but my heartbreak of losing in the hurdles was a greater pain to bear and I had no time to worry about my knees.

I ran the 400-meter dash, I didn't place, but I didn't care.
The hurdles were my *pride and joy*, and they are all that I cared about.
I didn't run the hurdles again until my knees healed.

It was towards the end of the track season when I met a girl from Riley middle school that ran the hurdles and she was bad.

She is light skinned, hazel eyes, she wore her hair in a long ponytail.

Returning from my devastating knee injury, and the first track meet back, she added more insult to my injury. She beat me not once, but twice in the hurdles before the season ended. It was a close victory, but nonetheless, she replaced me and took my number one ranking. I was no longer the top dawg.

It was our eighth-grade year and I never got the opportunity to redeem myself. I was moving on to high school and would never race her, again. My knee injury or maybe the thought that she was better than me caused many sleepless nights for me, the *competitor*.
I never got over the agony of her defeat.

𝄞 𝄞 𝄞

I excelled in sports and academics, and it was Emerson's awards night and the National Junior Honor Society ceremony time of the year. I was being inducted into the National Junior Honor Society for my academics on one night; the other night, I was acquiring awards for academics, perfect attendance, and sports.

I told my parents about both nights and how important it was for them to attend. I was giving a speech in place of Michael for the National Junior Honor Society ceremony because he was in a via bus accident. He was injured in the accident, so I was chosen to fill in for him.

My mother said that she wouldn't attend if Pee Tee and Della were going to be there. She didn't want to see them.

My dad didn't want to attend and see my mother and Alfred, either, but I think he only said that because my mother was adamant and said it first about not seeing him and Della. They both were acting very immature.

Awards night was special because it showed families all the hard work and dedication the student put in the entire school year.

I was going to receive awards and be inducted into the highest honors in middle school, the National Junior Honor Society, and my parents couldn't get along long enough to see their daughter honored.

I was hurt, not only hurt, I was torn because I wanted them to be proud of me and see how hard I worked, and for them to attend *both* ceremonies.

To get my parents to come, I chose which award night would be the most special and chose the parent I wanted to attend. They were both special nights and I couldn't choose one over the other, but neither parent would attend if they had to see each other.

I told my dad and Della to attend my Awards night, and my mom and Alfred could attend my National Junior Honor Society ceremony. They both agreed to attend on their respective nights.

Awards night was first, my dad and Della attended. I knew I was getting awards for academics, perfect attendance, and sports, but I had no idea what else if anything else.

To my surprise, I received about eight awards that night. It meant that I walked across the stage to receive awards ***eight*** different times. I received a trophy from Ms. Fees, my math teacher for a group science project that Tonya and I were in together. She received the same trophy. I received an award for homemaking; these awards were all surprises to me.

I was so happy and waved at my dad and family every time I walked across that stage. I couldn't stop smiling, I was overjoyed.
My dad was so proud of me.

I would never forget the look in his eyes each time he heard his daughter's name called for an award. Every time I walked across the stage, I looked directly at him. He was a proud dad and I could see him with his chest puffed out in his burgundy suit that he wore every time there was a major family event. In fact, it was the only suit that he owned.

It was the greatest night ever for me, but the sad part of my night was the fact that my mother missed it all.
She missed her daughter shining and glowing ***eight*** different times across the stage. A memory that I would forever treasure and never forget.

The induction into the National Junior Honor Society ceremony was nice and I got up there and didn't stumble on my speech like I thought I would. I did well, but that night couldn't compare to the Awards night that my father attended. I knew my dad would have enjoyed the induction into the noblest honor of middle school, too. I know he wanted to attend both ceremonies, but didn't because of what mama said.

I wished that my parents could have for two nights only, set their differences aside to see their daughter honored.
I took great pride in what I accomplished. I worked *hard* and I wanted to make my parents proud, especially my dad. I wanted them to be *proud* of me.

Chapter 6

Pipe Dreams

𝄞

My brother was the first to quit school among my siblings. He hung with Robert Lee running the streets and playing tardy each day. He was never into school ever since he was a little boy.

"James Campbell."
"James Campbell," Mr. Hornbeck my ninth-grade biology teacher announced twice.
I sat there listening to my teacher call my brother's name in my biology class.
Mr. Hornbeck proceeds with,
"Tammy Campbell."
"Present," I answered, proudly. I never wanted to be like my classmates, so whenever the teachers called the roll, I always answered, "present," instead of "here" like 99% of the class announced their presence.

Mr. Hornbeck continued to call my brothers' name each day to no avail. My brother was gone and wasn't coming back to school. I knew this but I didn't whisper a syllable.

My family's business belonged in the Campbells family. Our private business was private and our personal business was private.

It broke my dad's heart when my brother quit school in the ninth grade. He came to talk to my brother with tears in his eyes.

My parents both quit school in the eleventh grade, so according to my dad, it was important for us to acquire an education.

Even though, my dad didn't graduate from high school, he always held supervisor or manager positions in the workforce. He was the supervisor at Crest Haven Nursing Home. He was the manager of Church's Chicken on WW. White Rd, and he was the supervisor of maintenance at the State Hospital. He has always held managerial positions.

    We were getting older and no one could tell my sisters and brother anything. Our family was broken with no stability, and the ghetto was never kind in raising kids.
    My mom and Alfred's relationship was toxic, and we suffered from their constant arguments.
Their relationship was so bad that in 1985, my mother's family convinced her to leave him.

𝄞 𝄞 𝄞

    It was the summer of 1985 when we packed and left Alfred and Sutton J. Homes for the final time. I was fifteen years old, and Bobbie Jean and her kids were scattered in different homes. This was the *first* time that we have ever been apart from each other.
    My sister, Tina and her oldest daughter, Argentina, and my mother lived with my grandmother (My mother's mother). My brother moved with my dad and Della.
    My sister, Terrie lived with my aunt, Ruth Ann and I stayed with my aunt, Dorothy Nell; whom I consider my second mother. I often stayed with my aunt, Dorothy Nell and cousins, Roselyn, Rochelle, and Cedric each summer, so it made sense to continue to live with my aunt.
    My aunt lived on Dellcrest Street in the Dellcrest subdivision. She was a Licensed Vocational Nurse (LVN) at Santa Rosa hospital. I went to school at Fox Tech so she dropped me off at school on her way to work.
    My family and I didn't see each other as often as we would have liked, but this was the living arrangements and there wasn't much that any of us could do even if we didn't like it.

    My mother and Tina living with my grandmother wasn't the best but, thankfully, it was temporary.

    I was not happy living with my aunt, but I was not unhappy. I loved my aunt like a mother; she was a positive role model and took good care of me. She bought me school clothes and treated me like her *own* daughter. My aunt *loved* me. But I missed my family.

When visiting my dad, he would take me to my aunt's house and drop me off late as possible, and I know that he knew that I wanted to live with him, but Tina and her newborn daughter, and my brother was already living with him, Della, and her three kids.

I wanted to beg my daddy to please let me move in with him because I missed my family.

I sucked it up and kept my heartbreak to myself because he had a full house, and me living there would only add to his and Della's stressful relationship.

𝄞 𝄞 𝄞

Tina finally acquired her own apartment in the Wheatley Courts in July 1985 with her infant daughter and her boyfriend, Carl. Carl was one of my dad's friends.

My sister met Carl through my dad when she was pregnant with my niece, Argentina. My dad didn't like the fact that *his* friend was with his daughter. They fell out about it and they were no longer friends. It didn't stop Tina and Carl's relationship because she had two more kids with Carl; a daughter, Carla, and son, Carl Jr.

My mother had nowhere to turn, so she turned back to the only man that she knew, Alfred. She and Alfred moved in with my sister, Tina until my mother acquired her own apartment in the Wheatley Courts; AKA, The Wild, Wild, West. **The Ghetto**.

The Wheatley Courts were like a war zone; constant gunshots, drugs, hoes, pimps, drug dealers, police harassment and brutality, robberies, prostitution, burglaries. A bunch of black people that were going nowhere in life and the way the system was designed.

Black people killed each other in poverty or killed themselves physically and mentally with crack cocaine or drugs. No one had escaped the ghetto without scars or being damaged.
I said, No one.

𝄞 𝄞 𝄞

I turned sixteen years old in June of 1985, and I was still living with my aunt when my mother got her apartment in the Wild, Wild West. I was working at my first real job, Frank's Barbeque on W.W. White Rd.

I got the job because my aunt, Dorothy Nell wanted me to get a job since school ended.

I was awakened by the tone of my aunt's voice telling me to get up so that she could take me around to find a job. I was hired at Franks' that was located about three miles from my aunt's home. I made $2.00 an hour plus tips and free drinks. All that you could drink was on the house. We received a discount on food, too.

I was an immature mess when I worked at Franks. When there were no customers to serve, I'd go to the lobby, drink my soda, and sing-along with the music playing on the intercom in the restaurant. They played some old 60's & 70's sock hop white people "Happy Days" type of music. I still knew the songs because I loved all types of music, even white folk genres.

My manager always came to get me from the lobby to do certain unnecessary duties. He had me cleaning areas that needed to be cleaned; and at times, I had already cleaned.
I had no idea that when there were no customers, I couldn't sit down in the lobby and sing on the white man's time clock.

I made only $2.00 an hour. I felt like a slave on a plantation in the 1980's.

In fact, it was, but society made me feel like it wasn't slavery. It was the new and improved conditions of slavery called, "Underpaid employees."

𝄞 𝄞 𝄞

In August of 1985 is when my mother got her apartment at 101 Ira Aldridge located in the *heart of the ghetto*. I was still living with my aunt when my mother begged me to move back home with her. She wanted her family back. My aunt, Dorothy Nell was against me living in the Wheatley Courts and she told my mother that I could continue to live with her because she didn't want me in the projects. I agreed with my aunt and didn't want to live in the Wheatley Courts, but my mother was my weakness so I moved back home with her, Alfred, Terrie, and my brother.

Although, my brother was eighteen years old at the time and dating his children's mother, Freddie Mae and eventually moved in with her full-time. He wasn't home often before he finally moved out.

Where we lived, all criminal activities took place. We resided next to a bar called, The Corner Bar. And drunks, drug dealers, and everyone hung out at that location.

During this time, my father who was active and played basketball with my cousin, James and brother, was diagnosed with high blood pressure. I'm not sure if he ever took any medication for it, but he worked in construction with my uncle, Tommie when he bled from his rectum.
He joked about it, saying that he bled like he was having a period.
He was forty-one years old and in great shape, so it was nothing to be too concerned about since my dad joked about it.
He was in physically good condition and working, and when I was at his house over the summer, he made sure that the boy that lived in the back of his house stayed *far* away from me.
Rodney is his name and he loved him some me. It was puppy love, of course, but he always walked to the store and bought me a brown bag full of candy.
My brother and I played at his home a lot because he had sisters, and my brother was checking for them.

One day, we were on our way to my aunt, Debra's house, and I told my dad I wanted to stay home (at his house) and he knew I wanted to stay so that I could go to Rodney's house. He told me that I couldn't stay and for me to get in the car.
I got in the car that day, but there were plenty of summer days when my dad was at work and I was at Rodney's house.
There was nothing sexual between Rodney and me because I was too young, but we were two kids attracted to each other.
The attraction ended, and thanks to my cousin, Rochelle.
Rodney and my cousin went to school together and they were in the *same* seventh grade, and I was going to the eleventh grade. Even though, Rodney and I were the same age, he failed about three grade levels. When I found out, that was an immediate wrap.
Our puppy love relationship ends because I didn't want a *dumb* boyfriend.

On September 12, 1985, my dad was taken to University Hospital. I was at school and when I got home is when I heard that he was in the hospital. I talked to my brother on the phone since he was at the hospital with dad, and he informed me with the details of dad's condition. I asked if they need me to come to the hospital because I wanted to see daddy. I asked if dad's condition was serious and my brother assured me that it wasn't and that dad was up telling jokes and laughing. I don't know why I didn't ask to speak to dad, but I let my brother know to tell dad that I will catch the bus to the hospital in the morning the next day.

It was around midnight or later on September 13, 1985 when we heard Della knock on Tina's front door saying that the hospital called and that they want us all at the hospital *immediately.*

Della had a green 4 door Chevette Chevrolet and I have no idea how all of us fit into that small car.

We arrived at University hospital about thirty minutes or so later. There were white priests talking to Della and Tina. I don't know what they were saying because I was too busy asking God, not to let my father die.

I prayed in between all the commotion and priests, and my family's voices. It was a Twilight zone scene and my head was spinning. I prayed and prayed for my dad and I knew through my prayers that he would be healthy and back to normal.

He was too active and strong, and besides, he's only ***forty-one*** years old, and that's too young to die.

God, please don't take my father away from me. I begged as more commotion eluded the hospital waiting room.

Priests began to surround my brother and me while my sister and Della were in the room with dad.

I didn't want to be bothered with any priests. I wanted to go through the hospital's double doors that had a warning sign that read, "No Children Allowed in this area."

I wanted to bust through those doors, the hell with all the warning signs of "No Children Allowed."

I want my daddy!

The priests making all that ruckus and my concern for my father were getting to me...

And that's when I saw Tina coming down the hospital hallway crying with blood all over her clothes. It seemed like it took forever for her to reach us and everything was in slow motion. I watched Tina and the blood on her clothes at the same time. I don't know if I was more terrified of the blood on her clothes or what came out of her mouth...

"Daddyyyyyy isssss deaddddddd!"

I couldn't make out what my sister said because I saw Della throwing up as she ran inside of the bathroom. The priests and the bibles and Della were a temporary distraction of what I didn't want to hear.

"Whattttttt?!"

"Daddyyyyyy issssss deaddddd!" She was crying and devastated.

I screamed and cried at the top of my lungs. My prayers! My f*cking prayers were just that…

"F*cking *unanswered* prayers!"

My daddy, the man that I love is gone at forty-one years, two months, and twenty days old. I cried and cried. I was in disbelief. We all were in a state of shock.

I gathered the little strength that I had into my most devastating heartbreak to finally go into the hospital room and see my beloved father.

The warning sign of "No Children Allowed In This Area" no longer pertained to me. I was temporarily exempted and finally permitted in the area, and I was on my way to see my dad.

I got to my father's room and he lay naked on the hospital table with a white sheet across his body; his eyes closed with his mouth open that showed all his decayed teeth.

I didn't like the fact that his mouth was open; I went to his face to give him a kiss and told him that I loved him as my tears dropped onto his lifeless face.

I looked at his precious hand, the same hand that was smashed in the elevator when he worked at Dillard's in Windsor Park Mall in 1977.
It was the same year Terrie placed a hot iron against her face to see if the iron was hot.

The money we got from the Dillard's lawsuit when his hand was caught in the elevator was gone, but the scar remained on my father's hand until his death.

I looked and examined my father's body thoroughly. I don't know why his lifeless body became such an intriguing attraction for thorough analysis. I have seen him a million times throughout my sixteen years of life. Maybe it was my subconscious telling me that this was the last time that I would see him and that…
"My daddyyyyyy is deadddd!"
Why did you take my daddyyyyy awayyyyy?!
Nobody had an answer to my question or a solution for my endless pain. I was not only terrified of his unexpected death, I was beyond distraught. We were all traumatized.
My father's unexpected death made no sense to any of us.
One minute, he was laughing and joking, and the next minute, he was dead.
My dadddddddddy was gonnnnnnnne and he was not coming backkkkkk!
Dadddddddddyyyyyy, I lovvvve youu.

Chapter 7

Lost in the Blues

"Mama, daddy is dead," Tina said to my mother when she answered the knock on her front door.

We arrived at my mother's doorstep to wake her and tell her the bad news about daddy.
She couldn't believe it, and Alfred claimed the hospital had something to do with my dad's sudden death.
Alfred advised Tina to save the bloody clothes that she had on to get tested for any malpractices.

He insisted that there was something strange about my dad's sudden death. I felt the same way he did. I blamed not only the hospital, but I was angry at my brother for telling me that dad wasn't seriously ill.

My mother still legally married to my father didn't want to handle funeral arrangements, so she let my dad's sister, Debra handle the arrangements.
My dad had no life insurance and I don't know where we got the money to bury him.
He was buried a week after his death because we had to find burial money.
My dad's body began to smell. His casket was made from a cheap gray colored material that looked like concrete. His casket was the same cheap casket that my grandmother, my dad's mother who was murdered in 1984 during a home invasion was buried in. My aunt, Debra handled her funeral arrangements, too.
When we viewed my dad's body, he wore his one and only famous burgundy suit with his burgundy, white, and gray striped tie.
He looked peaceful, and in no more pain.
My daddy was at peace for once in his life.
I still cried for my daddy.

I cried because I was fatherless.
I cried because my siblings were fatherless.
I cried that I was not going to ever see my dad. And that this was the *final* time.

    I looked back at the memories, the good and bad, but the good is what I want to remember about my dad.
I loved *my* daddy.
I *needed* my daddy entering womanhood.
I needed my dad's protection and unconditional love.

    I took my dad's death hard. My grades reflected it. My GPA dropped to a 3.0.
I would cry every time it rained outside because my dad was in the ground in his casket and rain fell on him. I didn't want my dad hurt.
    My aunt, Dorothy Nell told me that it's okay to cry, it was my dad.
    I was growing up and coming of age, and at sixteen, I *need*ed my dad more than ever.
No matter what my dad was or wasn't, he was *still* my dad and he loved me, and I loved him.
But daddy was gone, forever.
Rest in peace, daddy. I love you.
James Edward Campbell Sr. (Pee Tee)
December 06, 1943- September 13, 1985.

Chapter 8

G.J.'s Blues

My senior year of high school in the summer of 1986 when I walked to Steve's store with pink rollers in my hair. I was the tender age of seventeen, and not too long ago I turned seventeen, and recently lost my beloved father. I saw him walking towards me as I crossed the street. I had no idea he would stop me.

"Heyyyy, what's your name?" He asked with the most beautiful smile.
"Tammy," I responded as I noticed his familiar face.
"I know you, you are Stephanie's brother. I was in cheerleading with your sister and we go to school together, Fox Tech."
A beautiful smile from ear to ear shines upon his face that lit the sunny morning sky. His smile has always been a trademark and was his number one attribute. He should have patented that unforgettable smile.
"Oh yeah, you know my sister?" How do you know me?" He asked as if I didn't know him but was in awe that I did.
"I used to go to your house when you lived in Second Baptist apartments." I didn't tell him that his sister, my cousin, and I was in his room doing things that we weren't supposed to be doing. We are six months apart from each other, his sister was eleven, I was twelve, and my cousin, Roselyn was thirteen.
One night, we went to play with his sister, and no, I'm not telling what we did.

Once we left his room, we went out back to the swimming pool. When we finished, we came back to Stephanie's room and she went to the kitchen to get us bananas. We ate the bananas and then she went into the bathroom to get toothpaste to mask what we'd done. We put the toothpaste on our finger and used our index finger like a toothbrush.

It was late at night when we snuck into the house so my aunt wouldn't smell us. We never did it again and told no one.

I confessed to my cousins that I liked the dark-skinned brother. I watched him come and go over the summer when I stayed with my cousins.

Roselyn liked the light-skinned, brother. I was glad she didn't like the dark-skinned brother so I could have him all to myself. He knew nothing about me as a little girl, but I *knew* him.

Five years later, the dark-skinned, brother stood in my face trying to get with me.
I stood there talking and embarrassed with big pink rollers in my hair. He was cheesing and asked for my digits.
I didn't give him my number because I was not allowed to have boyfriends until I graduated from high school. I let him know up front about my mother and her rules. These were rules that I never heard from my mother, but were sent by Tina when I was fourteen years old.

Tina told me that mama said I couldn't have any boyfriends until after graduation because she knew I liked a boy named, Terry from the Sutton Homes. I never questioned the authenticity of her message, I took it as truth.

He kept wanting to talk, but I cut it short, I was ready to go hide somewhere and get the rollers out of my hair.
He didn't care about pink rollers that day, he only cared about getting to know me. *All of me.*

Garland was his name but everyone called him, G.J.

He *loved* his name. When he told me his name, he said his *full* name. He often referred to himself in *third* person.

Tina went to school with him and they took homemaking together. She often talked about and liked him, too. She told me all these stories about what he did this day or that day in class. How he took a bite of her fried chicken that she cooked in class. She was thrilled, and I thought he was being greedy. Her stories of G.J. were told before I got with him.

She and Garland were the same age, but he was older by a few months. He was a star football player at Fox Tech high school. I don't recall what position he played, but I knew he was talented.

He is brown-skinned dark, 6'1 or 6'2, and weighed about 230lbs. He could pass for Steve McNair's brother. A very handsome guy that all the girls were crazy about.

"Oooohhhh, G.J." They would say.

I was seventeen and he was twenty-one when we first introduced ourselves. He owned two cars, a black Cadillac, and a 1968 Oldsmobile. His black Cadillac was his pride and joy, and the one he often drove. He called it, Caddy.

I guess he didn't get the message about me not allowed to have any boyfriends until graduation because he kept coming around my sister's house looking for me.

His persistent paid off because he and I became a couple.

We hung out mostly on the weekends in the beginning because I was in school during the day and worked part-time at Taco Bell after school.

We would go to the Drive-Inn movies and go cruising in the country and chill.

Every time he picked me up, he always asked if I had eaten. It was his second question after he asked how was school or how was my day. He always assumed that I was hungry. I know I was skinny but I wasn't necessarily *hungry*.

Except, one night, when we sat inside his caddy, after Tina came to mama's house to get me. She woke me up out of my sleep because G.J. wanted to see me. We communicated through my sister being the messenger so that my mother wouldn't find out about our relationship. *G.J. was twenty-one*. My mother wouldn't be happy with me dating a grown man. Trust me.

I got in the car and we were listening to the radio and that's when it happened.
My stomach started singing with the melodies on the radio. My stomach sang high pitched and out of tune, but nonetheless, it sang so loud.
G.J.'s head lies comfortably on my lap.

"Ut oh, somebody's hungry," he said.

"I just woke up, what do you expect?"
I tried to disguise my embarrassment. Besides, he didn't ask me if I was hungry and that was a rarity. Maybe he didn't have any money?
I doubt it because he *always* had money whenever he came around me.

The dark-skinned black men in the Wheatley Courts loved light skinned women and chased them like dogs in heat. When I moved into the courts, for some odd reason, I became the main attraction and the talk of the projects.

Men constantly harassed me ever since I moved into the courts. These were grown men chasing down a young me, and I was petrified. The men's behavior was something I wasn't accustomed to and I didn't experience this type of aggressiveness when we lived in the Sutton Homes.

There was this one guy named Willie, and he was twenty-five or twenty-six years old and his girlfriend's name was Rhonda. He was after me so bad that I told my mom. Willie lived across the pathway from where we stayed so she knew him and his girlfriend. One day, my mom saw Rhonda walking across the field on her way to Willie's house when she stopped her and told her to tell her man to leave her seventeen-year-old daughter alone. After that encounter, it was the last that I heard from Willie.

There was a drug dealer named, Peanut that paid teenagers to have sex with him.

He saw me one day and he was after me from that day forward. He was beyond aggressive and egotistical. His feelings were hurt when I rejected him that he came after me with a gun when I turned down his advancements.

I was *only* seventeen. What does a thirty-year-old man want with a seventeen-year-old girl? I rejected him and he was mad. But that made the two of us.

Peanut and his wife came to Taco Bell along with his kids a lot, and I would hide in the back until they left. Every time he came to Taco Bell, I hid.

I told my mother about Peanut, constantly after me, and I found out where he lived from a friend.

My mother and I went to talk to his wife. Mama brought her gun just in case she needed it. Her gun was like an American Express card, she never left home without it.

I don't know if the visit to his wife caused Peanut to back off or the fact that he knew I was dating G.J.

𝄞 𝄞 𝄞

The hood knew about G.J. and me, but my mother did not. I hid every aspect of our encounter from my mom. I told on every grown man, except, G.J.

When I started dating him, the men in the hood backed off, so I no longer had to run from them; instead, I ran into the arms of a man that was like the men that I tried to escape.

A few months into our courting, G.J. started pressuring me for sex. In fact, 99% of our disagreements were about sex. He needed sex and I was not giving him anything.

𝄞 𝄞 𝄞

One night, G.J. came to pick me up and we sat inside the caddy listening to the radio like we always did. He always wanted kisses, but I never gave him any. My mother told me that kissing leads to sex so that's why I didn't kiss him.

At times, when he drove his smaller car, the 1968 Oldsmobile, he teased me about the car being older than me, and he would let me drive. I didn't drive the caddy because it was too big.

I was learning to drive and I wanted to practice at each opportunity that presented me to drive, so I gave him a kiss and he would let me drive.

I'd give him a *quick* smooch, it was nothing long, but good enough to warrant me in the driver's seat. I did this a lot when he drove his 1968 Oldsmobile. He'd obliged each time.

It was the only way he got kisses from me.

We sat inside his caddy and G.J. became more and more intolerant and impatient with me not giving him *any* sexual satisfaction. He was sexually frustrated with me. He was a nice guy in the beginning and always embraced me with warm hugs and affection. I often sat on his lap like a little goofball so in love.

G.J.'s body was one that you could lie on top and fall fast asleep. He was protective and I knew that he would protect me from any harm, but months into the relationship, he changed. I still got the warm embraces but that wasn't enough for him.

We were dating for about six months and we were inside his Caddy listening to the radio and G.J. says,

"You see him? He points to his erected penis.

"Can you just touch him?" He asked.

"Noooo, I'm not doing that. What's wrong with you?"

"Nothing. I just want you to grab it." He grew more impatient.

"I'm not touching it, G.J." My eyes grew big and I became more terrified staring at his large manhood.

"Grab it got damn it! Do something!" He was beyond annoyed.

"No, No, I'm not touching it," I continuously told him.

"Why not, he won't bite."

"Because I don't want to, I already told you that I'm not touching it and I'm not ready for all that!" I cried out to him.

"You know what? Get out! Just get out! Get yo ass out! I gotta go get my dick wet!" He opened the car door and gave me a push out the door. I got out the car and he drove off mad as hell. He wasn't the only one mad because I was pissed.

He often begged his way back in after he'd throw a fit. I'd be walking down the street with my friends, chilling and having a good time, and he'd drive up beside us and tell me to, "Get in."
"Tammy, pleaseeeee, get in."
"I'm not trying to mess with you, tonight G.J., leave me alone." I would insist.

One minute, he wants to throw me out the car and the next minute, he wants me back in the car.

My friend, Markita didn't care for him because of the way he treated me. She often told me to leave his ass alone because I told her about him constantly pressuring me for sex and some of the things that he'd do to me.

I'd keep walking, ignoring him, but I knew that he would keep it up and ruin my night, so I'd obliged and got in the *damn* car.

He'd play all nice to get back on my good side and then when I'd let my guard down, he was back at it again. Same compassionate G.J. and then the overly sexed one. I never knew which one I would encounter on any given day.

As the relationship continued, he became more and more possessive. He would have it to where the minute I got into the caddy, I couldn't sit on my side of the car, the passenger's side, I'd have to sit right under him while he drove. If I would get in the car and not sit right under him, he would say,

"Where are you supposed to be?"

"Oh," I said and slid right where I was not supposed to be but did so to keep the peace.

𝄞 𝄞 𝄞

One night, we are driving to get Whataburger and G.J. starts, again. He *loved* scaring me by threatening to take me away from my mother.

"Get what you are going to get before we go to Vegas to get married," he said as we pulled up to the drive-thru of Whataburger.

"What? G.J. don't start; if you are going to trip, then just take me home. I'm too young to get married," I said in disbelief.

"We are going to get married so get whatever you are going to eat because you ain't seeing your mama no more."

He knew that I loved my mama with all my heart and the thought of not seeing her was imaginable.

"Take me home, G.J. I ain't playing with you. Take me home or else I will tell these people to call the police. You know that you ain't supposed to be with a seventeen-year-old," I threatened him.

"Ahhh, sit back and shut up and get your food."

I searched his face to see if he was crazy or deranged. I couldn't tell the difference, so he was probably both.

We got our food and then he took the freeway leading to an unfamiliar territory. He drove the freeway like he was taking me to Vegas because he knew that I didn't know directions, but I was happy to see the Kirby exit to where he lived. I was confused because I didn't know the area, but I was relieved to be heading towards his house and not Los Vegas away from my mother.

We got out the car with our food and he unlocked the door.
We encountered Stephanie and Gary.
 We greeted each other and G.J. told me to go to his room while he talked to Gary. I went to his room and turned on the T.V.
His brother was in his room blasting Cameo's "Candy" and "Word Up." G.J. stopped in his brother's room before he entered his room.

We were watching Friday night videos, eating, and talking. We finished eating and there was the little horny G.J. ready to spring into non-action because it wasn't happening and never was going to happen. If only he could realize it or maybe he didn't want to.
He starts his horny antics and was all over me trying to take off my shorts.

"Stop G.J.! Stop! Okay, okay, I have something to tell you," I told him to try to get him to stop and get his mind off sex.
He stopped and said, "What?"

"I'm embarrassed to tell you," I held my head down as I talked to him.

"What? You got a disease or something?"

"No, stupid," I snicker a little.

I was stalling and hoping that he would have mercy on me so I whisper,

"Ummmm, ummmm I'm a virgin."

"I know that! But don't worry because after tonight, you won't be," he said like my virginity was a *problem* and he could solve it.

I kept insisting him to stop, but he told me to be quiet before his mom came in the room. I would always get scared when he threatened about his mother. I never wanted to officially meet his mother, but I knew her from Emerson because she was always at Stephanie's cheerleading and sporting events.

"Get off me got damn it and stop!" as he continuously tried to pull down my shorts. There goes his raging hormones going wild.
He couldn't get my shorts down, so instead, he grinds on me until a white, yucky, slimy, and gooey gross liquid got all over my shorts and leg.

"Ewwwwwwwwww…. What is that, G.J.? What is wrong with you?"
He got up and went to the restroom and came back with a wet towel.

"What is wrong with you?" I kept asking him. It was different and I never experienced it before in my young seventeen years.

"Nothing, go to the restroom and clean yourself off." He gave me the towel and I got up and did what he said not knowing what was all over me. He never explained it so I had no idea.

I came back into the room a few minutes later, and he fell asleep. I was *glad* he was asleep so that I could watch Friday Night Videos in peace and he wouldn't bother me.

My favorite video was, "I Didn't Mean To Turn You On" by Cherrelle, and I always sang my jam, even though, the video was whack. Why would Cherrelle have a Gorilla as her love interest? The whole video was whack. I was so disappointed in the video but the song reminded me of G.J. and my relationship.

Often times, when I was at his house, he would fall asleep and I would be up watching T.V.

I'd watch him sleep, too because he was so gorgeous and I *loved* him. I thought back to how I watched him when I was twelve years old. Now, I have him in the flesh, right next to me.

     Week after week, this is what our relationship came to, the two personalities of a loving, kind man, to a sex crazed man. I didn't understand him or me for that matter. I was losing myself in him and the madness.

🎼 🎼 🎼

     We were in the Caddy one night and G.J. was deep in his thoughts.
     "I don't know if I love you or not because I ain't never had sex with you. How could you love someone but never had sex with them?" He asked himself.
I sat listening and not trying to interrupt his thoughts.
     "I don't know, Tammy but I'm *crazy* about you. I think it's infatuation. Yeah, that's what it is, infatuation."
He said infatuation like he was on Jeopardy and telling Alex that "infatuation" was his final answer.
     I thought to myself, "What does *infatuation* mean?"
I didn't ask him and didn't want him to think I was dumb because I was an honor roll student that didn't know the meaning of *infatuation*.
     The next day, I looked it up in the dictionary.

     I was not confused about my feeling for him. I loved G.J. ever since he lived in Second Baptist apartments. Of course, he was older and didn't know me, because he was in high school and dating Tracy.
     I never pondered my feeling for him, it was clear as day because I always wanted to be with him, *but not sexually*. When I was not with him, he was always on my mind.
     I would call into the radio station's "Party Line" and give G.J. a shout-out. I'd give my friends at Fox Tech a shout-out, too. I stayed on the "Party Line." The Party Line was a segment of the radio station where callers would call in and give shout-outs.
The radio host played the song, "Do you wanna go, partty. Have a funky time, parrrty"
     "This is the Party line. Who is this and who do you want to give a shout-out to?" The Deejay asked.

"This is Tammy, and I'd like to give a shout-out to G.J."

One day, he told me that he heard me on the radio and that I needed to be doing my homework, instead of playing on the radio. He made me mad when he treated me like a little girl, like he was my daddy. He loved when I gave him shout-outs because he'd ask if I was on the radio, and if I gave him a shout-out.

Sometimes I said, "yes," but one time, I told him "no, because I was doing my homework." He laughed hard at my comeback. I got him back for trying to act like my daddy.

I loved his laugh, it was so unique.

G.J. came to pick me up in my usual spot. We'd go get something to eat. It seemed like Whataburger was my favorite meal or his because we ate a lot of Whataburger's.

We finished eating and we were driving to the country to hang out. And his raging hormones were at it again.

"I'm taking you out to the country and raping you tonight," he told me.

"What?" G.J., you are crazy. You are not raping me. I will report you, if you do and I ain't playing," I emphasized vehemently.

"I am. You won't give it up like I asked you to." I've been waiting and waiting for months and you ain't trying to do nuttin. You are the only girl at Fox Tech that's a virgin. Everybody else is fucking."

"I don't care. I don't care what other girls are doing. Let them give it up. I'm not doing it."

He thought that I was supposed to feel like the lone ranger because all those other girls at school are screwing and I wasn't. He didn't know that that comment pissed me off and made me even more persistent in my stance.

"Is that all you think about is sex?"

"Yeah, I'm a man and I got needs, and you ain't giving it up so I'm just going to take it."

"Take me home. I already told you that I'm waiting for marriage. I'm not doing it."

I don't know why he didn't understand or want to understand nor respect my body or me.

"Take me home."

"Shut yo ass up. Get on my damn nerves."

"You get on my damn nerves too, always wanting sex." I clapped back at him.

"Shut yo ass up," he said as he raised his hand like he was going to back slap me if I didn't shut up. He never hit me, but he threatened to.

We continued to drive to the country and no more was said about sex that night.

We arrived at his mother's boyfriend, Chillie Willie's club in the country a short time later where he tried to pull me on the dance floor and dance to the song, "The Butt." I refused because I was not in the mood to dance.

G.J. grabbed this older lady with a big ole butt and they were out there dancing to the song, Da Butt.
He sang along, "Doing the Butt"

"Ain't nothing wrong. If you want to do the butt all night long." He danced like he didn't have a care in the world or what just happened on our way to the club wasn't wrong.

We were at G.J.'s house watching our favorite, Friday Night Videos. And he says out of the blue,

"You know what Tammy, you are going to always belong to me. I don't care if we aren't together, if I ever see you with another man. I'm going to beat his ass and slap the shit out of you. I don't care if I'm with my mama. I swear to God, I better not *ever* see you with another man," he emphasized with a guaranteed expression and adamant tone of voice.

When G.J. made this statement, it was confirmed that he was crazy and I was insane for being with him.

All my free time was spent with G.J; if I wasn't at school or work. I isolated myself from my friend, Markita to spend time with him. Markita complained about me always with him and how we don't hang out like we used to. I didn't think much of it. I wanted to spend time with him and hang with her, but I didn't know how to balance both. I had school and work, too.

The nice G.J. is back on this day.

The loving compassionate G.J.
The G.J. that I loved.
 He always embraced me with warmth and the gentlest hugs.
I swear, no one could give hugs like Garland.
Nobodddyyy.
I lived for his hugs, love, attention, and affection.
I wanted the same love from him that I got from my daddy, *unconditional love*.
He, at times, gave me that protection and unconditional love, and that was happiness.

"I got something for you," he said.
"Close your eyes and hold out your left hand."
I did what he asked. I had my hand turned with the palm facing upwards.
He turned my hand over with my palm facing down.
I feel him slide something on my ring finger.
I opened my eyes and there it sat on my finger. A tri-gold wedding band that was two sizes too big looped around my tiny ring finger.
I didn't know what to think. I knew that I was not marrying him because I was *too young* and the ring was too big.
    We drove to the store to get tape to make it fit. I think he was a little embarrassed because he didn't realize the ring would be so big.
    My ring finger was a size six and the ring was a size eight.
    He looped the tape around the ring and I kept taking the ring off and on, my finger, as he added tape to get the perfect fit. We got the correct measurement down to science, thanks to the tape. I looked at the ring and said, "Thank you" and how pretty it was. G.J. gave me a *beautiful* ring.
    I've never seen a tri-gold ring before and it was shiny and unique, and besides, it was from *my* boyfriend. We had been seeing each other for about seven months.
    "Don't you take it off, either."
The controlling G.J. was back for the moment.
    I didn't ask what the ring meant and he didn't tell me.
I hid the ring from my mama and my friends.
I didn't want anyone to think that I was married and my mama would have freaked out if she saw a wedding ring on my finger at seventeen years old. She didn't know anything about G.J. He was *my* little secret.

🎼 🎼 🎼

When G.J. picked me up from school, I would put the ring back on my finger like I had worn it the entire school day. I was too embarrassed to wear it to school because it was too big and it had tape to make it fit. I don't know why we didn't get it sized.
He never knew that I took the ring out of my purse and put it on as soon as he pulled up in the back of Fox Tech parking lot.

He would grab my hand to make sure the ring was on. He didn't peep on the cool. He let me know what he was doing and that the ring *needs* to stay on my finger.

He was always snooping in my business. Asking me if anyone was trying to hit on me at school.

"No," was always my answer and the right one. I know G.J. and there's *no way* I would mention anybody flirting with me. According to him, I belonged to him for life. I had a life sentence and I never committed a crime.

I think he felt a little insecure when it came to boys my age since he was a little older than me and had already graduated.

🎼 🎼 🎼

One day, when G.J. came to pick me up from school, it was my last class of the day when a classmate named, Chris wrote his phone number on my folder and when I got inside the car, it was the first thing G.J. saw. He saw the number *before* me. It was not a surprise because he noticed everything.

"Who the fuck is Chris?"

"Why are you asking me about him?"

He points to my folder and hits it kind of aggressively.

"Why the fuck is his number on your folder?"

"I don't know." I was telling the truth, I knew Chris liked me, but I didn't know he wrote his number on my folder. Chris was always trying to get with me asking me for my digits. He didn't know anything about G.J. I didn't tell anyone about G.J., except a *few* friends.
I would have scratched Chris' number off or hid it had I known he wrote it on my folder. The last thing I wanted to do was get G.J. riled up about someone that I had no interest in. ***I loved only him.***

"Tell that motherfucker that I said to come see me. O'le Punk ass nigga."

"Why? You're trippin. I got to go to work and I don't want to start nothing with you." He often picked me up from school because I mentioned that I didn't like walking or catching the bus to work so he'd come and pick me up so that I wouldn't have to catch the bus.

"Let that little nigga know that you don't want his number and you ain't available. Let me find out you messing with anybody and see what happens to him and you."

"You know what? I can just walk to work. I already told you that I don't know him and didn't know he wrote his number on my folder." I half ass lied. I knew Chris but the other part is true about him writing his number on my folder.

I went to school half a day and worked the other half of the day. I was in a program called, H.E.C.E.

I worked at Taco Bell on San Pedro and it wasn't too far from Fox Tech, but I didn't like walking or catching the bus, so G.J. often came to pick me up. Sometimes, he would have his cousin with him and I was not too fond of it, but I didn't complain, it was a *free* ride. I'm glad his cousin wasn't in the car the day he saw Chris's number on my folder.

G.J. was so jealous that it was pathetic. I was never insecure about him because he never looked or talked to any women in front of me. He didn't look at other women because he was too busy watching and *imagining* things about me.

One day, I wanted some candy so he pulled up to the corner store on Walters and E. Houston Street. He gave me money to go inside the corner store to get what I wanted. While I was in the store, I saw a classmate that already graduated and he greeted and asked me what I'd been up to.
I looked outside to see if G.J. was looking but I couldn't see him from my view until he swung open the corner store door and looked at me and said, "Are you done."
I was at the counter about to pay. Everyone at the front counter stopped and looked at G.J. It was like he stopped traffic.

"I'm about to pay, but yes, I'm done."

Ronald looked at G.J. and me and says, "Oh okay, Tammy, it was good seeing you."
G.J. closed the door and returned to his Caddy.
I don't know why he acted that way when he knew Ronald from school, too.
Ronald was in G.J's class or the class after his graduating class.
He didn't say, what's up or anything to him as if he didn't know him.

  I paid for my candy and awaited his pissed off wrath when I got in the car.
  "What the fuck was that all about?"
  "Oh nothing. I was just talking to him. We went to school together."
  "I don't care. I don't want you talking to no dudes."
  "I wasn't talking to him, I was just speaking and he asked me what I've been up to," I tried to explain.
  "You were all up in that nigga's face just a smiling and shit."
  "I always smile."
Smiling was my trademark, too, except when he made me cry.

  The ghetto had eyes and ears and it stayed in everyone's business without an invitation. The projects never slept and stayed open 24/7. It was like motel 6, it kept the lights on.
There were all kinds of rumors going around the Wheatley Courts about me that wasn't true.
  It was those grown men that I rejected that started the rumors. They were enraged about me turning them down and being with G.J. They didn't dare confront him or me, but one of his friends told him something about me and he brought it to my attention when we were at the Mission drive-inn.
  "You know Bobby K?" G.J. asked.
  "No, I don't know him, but I have heard of him. Why?"
  I knew Bobby but I didn't tell him how I knew him or mentioned that he tried to get my phone number, one day when he saw me at the store.
  "Because there's a rumor going around about you and that nigga that I know ain't true."

"Oh really? About me?" I ask in disbelief. Little ole me? I never mess with anybody why would anyone start a rumor about me? I thought to myself.

"Yeah, about you."

"What's the rumor? And who said it?"

"Oh nuttin, because I know it ain't true."

"Yeah, but I would still like to know." I wasn't going to stop questioning him until he told me.

"Nawww, I know that shit ain't true. Just drop it," he insisted.

"Oh, okay, if you know it ain't true, then what is it?" I wanted to know. He *finally* reluctantly told me.

"They talkin 'bout you gave Bobby some head, but shit, I know that ain't true, if we been together all this time and you ain't gave me no pussy, I know damn well you ain't givin no other nigga no head," he scarfed and huffed.

"What?" Who said that?" I wanted to know.
He said that Nutman told him.

"I know you know that ain't true."

"I know, that's why I didn't even want to bring it up to you."
I could tell that it bothered him even though he knew it was a lie.
He knew those jealous men wanted to sabotage our relationship.

They thought G.J. and I was having sex, but little did they know, we were hanging out together. Of course, no one knew about his raging hormones, but then again, that was nobody's business.
I kept it that way and so did he. Well, as far as I knew, he didn't tell anyone.

𝄞 𝄞 𝄞

My senior year of high school was flying by. I didn't mention the prom to G.J., but he brought it up at the last minute and asked if I wanted to go. I didn't want to go because I couldn't afford a prom dress and it was at the last minute, too.
I skipped the prom, but it didn't bother me because I didn't want to go anyway. I heard too many stories of girls losing their virginity on prom night. I was not trying to get caught up. I guarded my body with my life.

My friend, Erica and I were the last virgins of Fox Tech that I knew of until she got pregnant our senior year.

Erica and I became like salt and pepper the last year of high school. We were always together. I loved Erica like a sister. I would hang out a lot with my best friend, Nickki since Sutton J. Homes, but she became interested in a lot of things that I didn't want to partake in, so we grew apart, and Erica and I had more in common.

Nickki was my ride or die friend and was one of my friends that knew about G.J. When she first heard about him and me, she quickly told me that she knew his baby mama and that they were still together.
I knew G.J. had a son, but I *thought* his son was with Tracy. I knew of their relationship because he told me that I reminded him of her and that he loved her.
I didn't know his son was with another girl named, Wendy.

Nickki brought the pictures to school a few days later of G.J. and Wendy. It was during Christmas time and she was pregnant.
I told Nickki that I know he has a son, but I had no idea about him still together with his baby mama. How is he with me all the time, how could he be with his baby mama?
What time was he giving her when he was giving it all to me?
He was always horny, too. If he had another woman then why did he pressure me for sex so much?
The pictures broke my heart. "*My* G.J." was messing around on me and was still in a relationship with his baby mama.
The day I saw the pictures, he picked me up from school. You know I let him have it as soon as I got into the car.
"Are you cheating on me?"
"What the fuck are you talking about?"
"You know what I'm talking about. I know that you have a son, but are you still with your child's mother?"
"Hell nawwwwww. I go by and see my son and that's about it."
"You are lying. My friend, Nickki showed me pictures of you and her when she was pregnant with your son."
"Wait a minute. Who da fuck is Nickki?" He hissed.
"Nickki is my friend," I hissed back at his ass.
"I don't know no damn Nickki. Who da fuck is Nickki? He kept asking and insisting that he doesn't know no damn Nickki."

"Mannnn, you letting your little friends that don't even know me fill your head with bullshit."

"Look, I go by and see my son, but you already know about my son," he continued to explain.

I didn't know what to believe because how the hell could he have a woman when he spends all of his time with me? If I'm not at school or work, I'm with him.
I was hurt, confused, and angry all rolled into one.

We never brought up Wendy again, but I paid more attention to his damn whereabouts than before.

𝄞 𝄞 𝄞

The Fox Tech class of 1987 graduation was upon us, it seemed like I saw a little bit less of G.J., but I didn't notice because I was getting ready to graduate. It wouldn't be too long before I was going into the Air Force to buy my mother her dream home.

Whatever he was doing wasn't my priority or concern, lately. He wore me down with his raging hormones and it was a breath of fresh air not to deal with him.

One of my brother's friends,' Darryl was checking me out, but it wasn't even like that because G.J. was *my* heart and he knew it. We were not on the same page when it came to that dreaded three letter word, ***sex***. I'd been dealing with him for eight months. I couldn't believe that I put up with him for sooooo long.
I couldn't believe *we* put up with each other.

𝄞 𝄞 𝄞

My grades weren't what they should have been. I was disappointed that I was not being inducted into the National Honor Society. My GPA was a 3.33 and I needed a 3.5.

My GPA took a nose dive when I worked at Jeepers fast food restaurant on N. New Braunfels Street.

In the H.E.C.E program, students must maintain a job because employment made up 50% of the grade.

One day, I was at work and the manager who was dating another employee asked me if I could work a double shift because he was getting off work, and his girlfriend shift was beginning, but she wanted to leave with him, so he tried to make me work her shift. I told him that I couldn't work a double and that my mother was outside waiting for me. He told me that I needed to work and that I *better* not leave. Why did he tell me that? I told him that the only thing that I *better* do is, live and die and stay my color, and I walked out.

    The word got back to my teacher that I didn't have a job, and there were only two people that knew that I quit, the manager and a "friend." I won't name any names, but I have a strong feeling who told my teacher and it wasn't the manager.
    My plan was to hurry and get a job before my teacher found out that I quit. The little snitch got to my teacher first and told my teacher that I didn't have a job, but instead of Mrs. Sutton giving me an "F," she gave me a "D" and it tanked my GPA.
    I recently loss my dad, so I was in mourning and my grades reflected it.
    I was not selected for the National Honor Society. It hurt that I didn't make it in high school. I forgave the person that told my teacher but, don't think for one second, I didn't know who told.
    I was grateful that Mrs. Sutton didn't give me an "F" because she was supposed to. I think she liked me as a student because I would always sit right next to her when she turned off the lights to show videos.
    The boys in my class were nasty and they sat in the back of the class to feel all over the girls once the teacher turned off the lights and started the video.
    The girls wore skirts on those days to give the boys easier access. They made a beeline to the back of the classroom with the nasty boys. A few of my friends would go to the back of the classroom so the boys could feel on them. The boys tried to pull that feeling on me but, I was not going for it. I'd sat right next to Mrs. Sutton to make sure no one touched me. I think Mrs. Sutton knew what was going on but didn't say anything.
    The nasty boys laughed at me and called me, scary. It wasn't about being scary, I didn't want *anybody* touching me. I was never a fast tail.
Some of my friends laughed at me. It's all good, though, because, you couldn't back then and still can't touch me. Hammer Time.

🎼 🎼 🎼

I had a little crush on my government teacher, Mr. Tyler. He was nice looking and he taught government and economics.

There was a guy in my class named, Billy. He played sports and he never had time to study, so he would ask to cheat off my test. We had scantrons and I would put my scantron at the edge of my desk so that he could see it. I told him to make sure he changed some of his answers and don't put the exact answers as me. He agreed and this was our understood agreement.

One day, we get our test results back and Billy received a 90% and I got an 88%. I was shocked and asked him, "How did you make a better grade than me when you cheated off me?"

We laughed about how he made a higher grade than me, and to this day, I still don't know how he did it. I must have erased a few answers I wasn't sure about and he saw the eraser markings, and those were the answers he changed.

I will never forget the day Billy got a higher grade than me. I think Mr. Tyler knew that Billy often cheated off my tests, but didn't want to get me in trouble along with him.

Mr. Tyler often asked me to take papers to the main office and I would melt all inside.
He could be my government and politician *at any time* and I loved running errands for him.
Mr. Tyler was my teacher crush my senior year.
But, Shhhhhh don't tell G.J.

🎼 🎼 🎼

Graduation night had come and no word from G.J. He knew our graduation date; he knew our graduation theme song; he knew when we were taking our graduation pictures; he knew everything about our class because his sister told him. He knew more about the class of 1987 than I did. He asked about my class ring and I told him that I ordered it from Shaw's jewelry and I was making payments. He said he would finish the payments. He made ONE payment, maybe two at the most, but that was it. I paid it off.

One day, G.J. and I were looking at my senior class group picture and he asked who my friend, Elaine is. He tried to get me jealous but it didn't work.

"Oh she lives on E.Houston Street and she may be willing to give you some." I laughed. He took the rolled up panoramic group picture and playfully popped me on top of my head with it. He wasn't interested in her and tried to get me riled up. I didn't fall for it. His plan failed, miserably.

G.J. *never* looked at other women in front of me or made me feel insecure.

𝄞 𝄞 𝄞

The graduation ceremony ends. The class of 1987 was in the record books and I was officially a high school graduate. My family was in attendance along with my grandmother, aunts, and uncle. I would have loved for my dad to see me walk across the stage.

Tammy age 17 (Fox Tech High School) Class of 1987

    I was the first to graduate in my family, but it was not a big deal to me. It was a milestone that I needed to reach to get to the next milestone.

    My friend, Erica wanted to go out to celebrate, but I was not in the mood. I had not heard or spoke to G.J. I was a little down and not feeling any happiness. Especially, after what Tina whispered to me that G.J. was in attendance and how he tried to hide from her but she saw him. He was sitting with his mama and there was a girl there, too. She though it was his baby mama. She nor I have never seen her.

    My heart skipped two beats and it took everything in me not to cry as I smiled for the pictures trying to mask my disappointment. This was my graduation night and my 'boyfriend' disappeared into thin air.

I didn't see G.J. for months after graduation.
No call and out of sight.
The only thing he left was a band of gold wedding ring that I kept hidden. I was a sick puppy and distraught. I kept thinking if I'd only given it up, he wouldn't have left me.

One night, I was looking out my bedroom window and saw G.J.'s Caddy, I thought I would get a message from my sister and she'd come get me, but no, instead, he stopped by Nutman's house who lived right across the pathway from my house, and he got into his Caddy and drove off.

𝄞 𝄞 𝄞

It was almost a year since I heard from G.J. I was *all* cried out over him and moved on and started dating my brother's friend, Darryl who liked and cherished me.
He adored me so much that it became an obsession.
 Darryl wasn't the only man that adored me.
Willie's brother, Greg, who was dating a girl named, Theresa was on the prowl since he no longer saw G.J. around. Greg was eight years older than me and Theresa was a few years younger than him.

The dogs started coming back out of the woodworks. G.J. held them off and now he was gone and the dog packs were back.

I pawned the wedding ring that G.J. gave me. I needed the money and besides, I was not married and the ring was no use to me. He left me so I moved on with my life.
I was dating Darryl.

Darryl and my relationship was still fresh and new when Greg offered to give my sister and me a ride to H.E.B on New Braunfels Street. I stayed in the car to wait for my sister to run in the store to get what she needed.

Greg, who drank beer every day tried to kiss me. I fought him off and told him to quit.

"Aww, come on Tammy don't be like that, just give me a little kiss," he begged as he puckered his peeling burnt red lips. He drank so much that the alcohol turned his lips, brown and red.

"Greg, gone on, you have a girlfriend and I have a boyfriend."

"Aww she won't know unless you tell her."

He continued trying to kiss me as I tried to fight him off, and when it was over, said, and done, my lipstick got on his white polo shirt.

Tina came out of the store and got into the car, she knew something was up with Greg but didn't say anything.

He dropped us off at my sister's apartment, and as soon as we got out the car, we saw Diane, who is Greg's sister, and she was also Greg's girlfriend, Theresa's friend.

𝄞 𝄞 𝄞

Later that night, I was walking home with my boyfriend, Darryl when Theresa and her sister, Sabrina, and Diane approached me.

"Tammy, I heard that you were in the car with Greg and you kissed him," Theresa said with a stank attitude.

"I didn't kiss Greg. Greg tried to kiss me," were the last words that came out of my mouth before I felt a hard slap across my face. I saw Lucky Charms' cereal, stars, clobbers, moons, and diamonds; the whole entire rainbow when she slapped me. Theresa slapped me so hard that she slapped me back into last week, last month, and last year.

What the fuck did she do that for? Does she know who she is fucking with? She didn't know until that night that I had a little crazy in me.

My tongue curled underneath my teeth and I struck. I struck hard, too.

I grabbed her by her hair and threw her on the ground like a sumo wrestler. I took her head and repeatedly beat and punched her with all the rings that I wore on my right hand. I wore a lot of jewelry during that time. My rings were like brass knuckles going upside her damn head. I punched her left eye until I couldn't punch anymore. I beat her head into the concrete until I couldn't beat it anymore. I turned into the incredible hulk. She didn't like me when I was angry.

I went into a rage and I couldn't stop beating her.
It was so bad that my sister, Terrie tried to stop me but I wouldn't stop. Terrie ran home to get mama before I killed Theresa.

"Pow, Pow" was all that stopped me. I didn't know who was shooting or even if I was the one being shot at or shot. My adrenaline was in overdrive and I didn't feel anything. The hits that I took from Sabrina on my back, I never knew occurred until my sister, Terrie told me. She grabbed Sabrina off my back.

When the shots rang out, it was like I had been shot because the sounds of the gunfire were all that resonated with me that night.
And the fact that Theresa slapped me into oblivion in front of my boyfriend. I tried to kill her ass.

I stopped when I heard the shots. I got up off Theresa's ass and as I looked around in a daze, I saw the entire Wheatley courts standing and witnessing Theresa's beat down.

There stood my mama with her gun. She was the one that stopped me and saved Theresa's life as well as mine.

Murder would be the case that they gave me had my mom not come to our rescue.

Dead on arrival would have been Theresa's faith.

I looked around for my boyfriend, Darryl but he was nowhere to be found.

My mother took me home to cool off because I was heated.

I didn't hear from my boyfriend until the next day.
I asked why he'd left and he said that he wasn't going to stand around and watch me fight over another man.

"Are you serious? I am not fighting over no damn man. I was fighting because that b*tch came up and slapped me. Did you not see her slap me?" I couldn't believe his reasoning and I felt betrayed by his abrupt disappearance.

𝄞 𝄞 𝄞

I saw Theresa the next day on her balcony, and her left eye had a patch on it, and her head was wrapped in a white bandage. I didn't know what her prognosis was but she knew that Tammy Campbell was the last person that she would ever mess with. Her prescription from the doctor should have read, "Stay the hell away from Tammy Campbell stat!" If I had to guess her diagnosis, she had to have a concussion and a few black eyes because that was where most of the punches landed. I didn't know and I didn't give a damn. I Floyd Mayweathered her ass because she slapped me, hard.

There were rumors of Theresa's sister, Sabrina and Diane jumping me.
I carried a switchblade and dared each one of them to bring it.
They never brought it like I thought; all talk and no action. They knew exactly where to find me. In the hood. Where I resided for two miserable years. I don't know why I didn't go back to live with my aunt because I *hated* the hood.

The project chicks had an up close and personal view of how I stomped Theresa's ass into that concrete and they wanted no part of me.
I didn't want any part of me.
I didn't know this young lady that I had become.

A young girl (me) that once upon a time was sweet, smart, and innocent, had turned into the environment I grew accustomed to, *the ghetto*.

Chapter 9

The Lonely Blues

𝄞

My boyfriend, Darryl was interesting and weird in a peculiar way. He was dark, medium height, and muscular. He had a baby face. He resembled the rappers, Too Short and Jay Z rolled into one person.

I was eighteen years old and he was twenty when he and I began to date.

I don't know why I got involved with Darryl. I'm not sure if it was a rebound effect to purge G.J. from my system or he was convenient. He was always available and I was *kind of* feeling him.

In the beginning of our relationship, it was great, but I couldn't take his jealousy as the relationship progressed. He watched me like a hawk. If you think G.J. was jealous, Darryl took the entire cake.

He was a master at kissing. The brother could kiss your bra and panties right off you.

Our entire relationship was mostly kissing. His lips were so soft, juicy, and kissable.

Darryl and I were not dating long when G.J. showed up one night when we were outside talking and walking towards the apartment. I haven't seen G.J. in *almost* a year. It was like eight months, but still, that's *almost* a year.

It was dark and he came from out of nowhere like he had been watching us.

Darryl and I were going to my house to sit on the stairs to talk and of course, *kiss*.

I saw G.J. walking towards us and we continued to walk getting closer to my home. I kept thinking, I hope G.J. doesn't say anything to Darryl or me.

Darryl wasn't aware of G.J. and my relationship, and I didn't discuss him so he had no idea why G.J. was walking towards us.

"Tammy, can I talk to you?" G.J. asked.

"Yeah, hold on one minute."

"Darryl, can you wait for me on the stairs, I'm going to see what he wants," I whispered to Darryl.

I don't know why Darryl didn't ask any questions, he did what I asked. I walked closer to G.J. to see what he wanted.

Darryl was *my man*. G.J. left me but he comes back on the scene and there I stood talking to him while Darryl waited for me on the stairs of the apartment.

"Tammy, who is that nigga?" G.J. inquired.

"He's my friend. Why?"

"What kind of friend?"

"Wait, you been gone for almost a year and you have the nerve to ask me who he is? I questioned him feeling irritated.

"I want you to go with me," he said.

"G.J., you just can't waltz back into my life and expect me to drop everything to be with you."

"I want you back."

"You see me with someone else. You don't want me. I gotta go," I said and left him standing there as I walked around the corner where Darryl waited for me.

G.J. walked after me and came around the corner to ask Darryl who he was. He had *some* nerve. Darryl didn't answer and I already told him who he was and besides, it wasn't any of his *damn* business.

"G.J., *you* need to leave." I insisted.

If looks could kill, Darryl would have died right in my arms that night. Darryl didn't budge and G.J. felt the wrath of a man that didn't care how much bigger he was than him. If he didn't leave there would be trouble.

Fortunately, and thank God, G.J. left after he saw that I wasn't going with him, and chose to stay there with Darryl, my *new* man.

"I know that nigga," Darryl said.

"He was dating a girl that worked with me at Popeye's on W.W. White rd. She always talked about him and how he did her wrong. Her name is Wendy but they call her, Lou," Darryl explained. This would be the second time that I heard the name, Wendy. I explained to Darryl about G.J. and my relationship since he brought his ass around and made a scene.

"He and I used to talk but he left me almost a year ago, and I don't know why he's back."

"Why did you go and talk to him and leave me here?" "You still want to be with him?"

"No, I don't want him starting anything."

"I ain't scared of that nigga. Tammy, you ain't messin with no punk.

"I know, but I don't want no mess and I didn't want to wake up my mama, either."

Darryl was upset but tried not to show it. There was no kissing that night. He left a little after G.J.

Darryl knew that I *still* loved G.J. and the reason he left.

G.J. ruined our night.

𝄞 𝄞 𝄞

I spent a lot of time at work after graduation. My dream of joining the US Air Force and moving my mother out of the courts faltered because mama didn't want me to leave. She said that I could go to school here and not have to go in the service. I wanted my mother out of the projects fast, but I reluctantly did what she asked of me.

I loathed the Wheatley Courts, so I didn't mind working full-time at Taco Bell to get away from the environment. I was promoted to a Shift Manager as soon as I acquired my driver's license.

One night, I was at work and I heard a man say, "Go get your manager, NOW!" I saw a black man holding a gun to my co-workers' Michelle's face.

I was in the back of the store cleaning and getting ready to shut everything down for closing when I saw the gun. I immediately got on the floor in a hidden position.

Michelle called out the manager's name,

"Erickkkkk, somebody wants to see youuuuu." She said with trepidation in her voice.

I stayed on the ground as my manager walked passed me and smirked and said, "Ms. Tammy what are you doing on that floor?" He continued walking to see why Michelle called him and why I was on 'that' floor.

He walked up to the front and said, "ewwww" in his gay feminine dialogue, as he saw a gun pointed at him and the robber barking out instructions to give him all the motherfucking money in the register, including the money in the safe!

"Where is that other girl at? Tell her I said to come up front!" The robber insisted.

He was talking about *me*, but how did he see me? I got on the floor as soon as I heard his voice and saw him pull the gun on Michelle. I was scared senseless, but I knew that if I didn't get my ass to the front that I could put my co-workers' lives in danger. I could have locked myself in the freezer or even ran out the back door. Reality told me to do so but my feet wouldn't let me risk it.

I reluctantly stood up and slowly walked to the front of the store without Erick or Michelle telling me. I heard the robber's commands and I obliged.

As I got to the front register, he shouted,

"Get your ass on the floor before I blow your fucking head off!" He had a serious demonic look in his eyes.

He pointed the gun directly at my head as I slowly got on my knees with my hands raised in the air. He didn't tell me to put my hands up, but I did just in case he wanted me to. I watched robbery victims on T.V. so I did what they did. I didn't take my eyes off the gun and I must have died instantly looking up at the barrel.

I was revived and resuscitated when Erick hands the robber the bag of money as he ran out Taco Bell's front double door entrance. The doors facing Pizza hut's restaurant.

I worked for Taco Bell ever since I was sixteen years old and in high school, and I have never been robbed at gunpoint. I only saw robberies in movies not in real life, but oh no, what I experienced was not a dream nor a movie, *it was real life.*

Erick asked if we were okay; we were not physically harmed, but mentally, we were all over the place. Michelle ate packets of sugar to calm down and I walked around like a deer in headlights.

Erick was a gay black man, and he was the calmest of us three, as if robberies were something he was accustomed to.

He called the police and we each gave a statement about what happened.

Erick instructed us not to give the police the amount of money that was taken and we agreed.

But how would we know the amount of money that was taken when *he* was solely in charge of the money that night? We hadn't cashed out the registers so how would Michelle and I know the amount of money in the bag? I didn't question anything, and his comment seemed logical at the time. I would have agreed to anything while being in a state of shock.

I drove home that night shaken.
I was upset at my mother so I never told her about the robbery.
Darryl was at my house to comfort me and I told him about my night.
I swore that I would never work the night shift at Taco Bell.

We were questioned a few days later by the police as they showed mugshots of criminals to help identify the robber or robbers.

The police suspected that the robbers were twin brothers. They were dark-skinned with nappy hair that resided on Virginia Street located on the eastside.
I identified through mugshots who I thought robbed Taco Bell, and the man that sat in the lobby prior to the robbery.

One brother ate inside the restaurant to see how many employees were working that night, while the other brother came in and robbed us.

As far as the criminal aspect, I never knew the verdict; it was shocking that my own black people were willing to commit a crime or even kill me over money. I thought *we* were all family?
I was acquiring money the legal way, and the robbers wanted money the easy way.

𝄞 𝄞 𝄞

I owned a 1979 Pontiac Grand Prix that I bought with my student loan money. I attended San Antonio College in the Fall of 1987. I didn't have a driver's license, so my mother drove my car. She dropped me off and picked me up from school. I had one-night class, and after class would end, I'd go to the SAC center with a cool Mexican girl, and she and I would shoot pool.

She was cooler than a fan. She carried a thermos and took many trips to the bathroom during class.

I later discovered that she was an alcoholic. She didn't let it interfere with her school.

Every time after class, she'd ask if I wanted to shoot pool and offered me a drink from her thermos. I always refused. I didn't drink and I wasn't drinking after anyone.
Sometimes, we played video games.

I asked my mom to pick me up a little later so that I could stay after class and shoot pool.

Darryl often asked my mother if he could ride with her to pick me up.
I'd hate when he came because he would always have a stank attitude and think I'd stayed after class to shoot pool with other men.

He'd give me the meanest look that scared me. Darryl was never violent with me, except for one night when he and I were outside and he kept chasing me. We were playing a cat and mouse game.

He'd catch me and then we would kiss, and I'd take off running. He continued to chase and catch me, and we'd kiss, and I would take off running, again. The game continued in this fashion. When it was time to kiss, he kept kissing me and feeling all over my body trying to take it further, and I told him to stop but he wouldn't.

I took my knee and hit him in his balls and took off running.
He dropped to his knees as he held his balls.
After he caught his breath, he came after me.

"I told you to stop, but you wouldn't!" I explained to him.
He looked at me without saying *one* word and came closer to me and slapped my face.
I was shocked and hurt. It wasn't a hard slap and wasn't close to the slap that Theresa gave me, but it was *still* a slap.

I grabbed my face and yelled that I never wanted to see him, again.
He tried to explain how sorry he was and that kicking him in his balls hurt.
I ignored him and went upstairs.
I didn't tell my mother what he did because I didn't want her to shoot him. I decided that I was not going to see him, anymore.

Two days had passed and Darryl kept looking for me and I ignored him. I wanted *nothing* to do with him.

One morning, he came riding a bike, around and around my house at five am for about an hour screaming,
"Tammyyyyy, I'mmmmm sorryyyyyyyy!"
"Tammyyyyy, I love youuuuuuuuuuu!"
Each time he passed my house, he would alternate saying those words.
My mother was the first to hear him because I was asleep. My mama told me that he's crazy and that I need to leave him alone.
She never asked what happened between us and I didn't tell her.

It was a few weeks that I didn't talk to Darryl and truth be told, as crazy as it may sound, I missed him and tried to formulate a *good* reason to go back to him after the slap.
The illogical reason that I regurgitated over my conscious mind was that I hit him in the balls so what would I expect to happen?

Darryl and I got back together and he never laid *one* finger on me. Stop meant stop, and he never pulled that feeling all over me, again.
Darryl and I were together for about eight months before he got arrested for violating his probation.
I never knew he was on probation and didn't know why.

🎼 🎼 🎼

Darryl never pressured me for sex like G.J. We waited for eight months until with took the relationship to the next level. Two nights before he went to jail is the night I **supposedly** lost my "virginity."
We were at the Mission Drive Inn.
I was eighteen years old, and we were kissing and it went a little too far.
Darryl pulled down my underwear and tried to put his penis inside of me. It hurt like hell, so I reached down and scratched his penis.
"Ouchhhhhhhhh!" He said as he grabbed his penis.
He *immediately* stopped and got off me.
He put the tip of his penis at the entrance of my vagina and I scratched him and it was over that quick.
"Does this mean that I'm not a virgin, anymore?" I asked with disbelief in my face and voice.
"Yeah, and don't tell your mama," he said in a nervous voice.

Everybody was afraid of my mama because they knew that I was her favorite and she told everyone not to mess with *her* Tammy.

I didn't know if I was still a virgin or not because we didn't do anything. He wanted to be my first and so what we did was close enough to being the first.

I didn't tell my mom what we did and went into my room and stayed there with disappointment that I was no longer a virgin.

Darryl came by my house the next day to see me, but I told my mother that I didn't want to see him.

I started my period and I was still in shock and confused about what happened the night before at the drive in. I was too embarrassed to face him.

We did the nasty or did we? I was confused about everything. I was *half* a virgin. I guess.

When I finally came out to talk to him two days later, we sat in my car when the policeman that many called, Red pulled up to my car and arrested Darryl.

I was distraught and didn't know why he was being arrested. Red said that it could be a misunderstanding and that Darryl needs to go downtown and clear it up. And that he will return soon.

Hours later, I received a call from Darryl saying that he was staying in jail and being sent to prison.

Prison? What the hell?

𝄞 𝄞 𝄞

It was the Spring semester of 1988 when I withdrew from San Antonio College.

In the Fall of 1987, I was going to school full-time and barely sustained a 2.5 GPA.

These low grades were unheard of for me since I'd always been an honor roll student.

My grades plummeted even more the following semester. Classes were more challenging and I lacked focus.

I attended college to become a Registered Nurse (RN). The profession that my father chose for me.

The day when my dad told me he wanted me to be a nurse, I was thirteen or fourteen years old, and we are at Sutton and Sutton funeral home viewing Little Boy's body.

Little Boy always came to our home on F. Street and he'd bring my baby sister cookies. He *never* brought Tina, Edward, or me any cookies. I mean, we liked cookies, too. My baby sister was stingy with her cookies, until one day, mama and daddy got their income tax check refund.

Mama taught Terrie about the meaning of "checks and money." She'd tell Terrie that when there was a check in the mail then that meant, it's money, but when there was no check in the mail, then that meant, no money.

Mama would say, "check."
And Terrie would say, "money."
And mama would reply, "no check."
Terrie would shake her head side to side meaning, no, and respond, "nooooooo money."
We laughed all the time when my sister did this.
She was only five years old.

We would run to the mailbox every day looking for our parent's income tax check. Mama said that the income tax check was in a gold envelope with the Statue of Liberty printed on it.
On this day when Little Boy showed up and brought Terrie her cookies. She knew the check came in the mail and she started giving us *all* her cookies.

𝄞 𝄞 𝄞

My dad told me that he wanted me to be a Registered Nurse. I didn't want to let my father down, but everything was taking its toll on me, so I quit school because
poverty,
my father's death,
Darryl's absence,
G.J.'s inconsistent presence,
my loneliness,
the uncertainties of tomorrow living
in the Ghetto was too overwhelming.

I reasoned with myself that I would *only* take a semester off to get back on track and get rid of the distractions in my life. I'd return next semester and become the honor student that I used to be. It never turned out how I planned, but life never does without throwing a curve, breaking, and slider balls.

𝄞 𝄞 𝄞

Shortly after Darryl's arrest, G.J. showed back up on the scene.

I *knew* that someone was watching me closely and told G.J. my every move. There was no way that his unexpected visits weren't planned.

The reason I knew was because when I started dating Darryl, G.J. showed up after being gone for almost a year. It was eight months, but still, that's *almost* a year.

Darryl goes to jail and here's G.J., again.

He had an informant that kept tabs on me.

Someone with no life.

G.J. came to me one night in the courts to see if he and I could get back together. He didn't ask about Darryl because I'm sure he already knew that he was in jail. His secret informant couldn't keep that pertinent information from him.

I resisted G.J. at first, but then I relented because I was *lonely and I still loved him.*

"Why did you just up and leave me?" I always wanted to know.

"Tammy, I didn't want to taint you and mess up your life. I was doing shit that I wasn't supposed to be doing and you were a good girl, and I wasn't right for you at that time."

"So, leaving me and going away for almost a year was the right thing to do?"

"Tammy, I messed up, can we just put it behind us and try again?"

"You hurt me," I said.

I loved G.J., and as much as I tried to resist him, he'd draw me back in. He always called me his 'good girl.' Meaning, I was innocent and green and could easily be taken advantage of in the courts.

What a *lame* ass excuse that he sold and I bought.

Darryl was locked up and I had fallen for him, but G.J. **always** held a special place in my heart.

G.J. and I was back together in 1988.

It was beautiful again, in the beginning like when I was seventeen, but it didn't take long before the real G.J. was back.

He asked about the ring he gave me and I told him the truth that I pawned it because he left, and why would I want the ring? He was disappointed that I pawned it and asked how long ago and maybe we could get it out. He wanted to know the pawn shop and wanted the pawn ticket as well.
I told him that I pawned it a little after he left and that the ring was lost.

G.J. and I were hanging out strong, the relationship was going well, so I decided to give him what he wanted for over two years. It was still not on my own merit and I felt forced. If it was up to me, I could have waited longer.

I was **half** a virgin because it hurt like hell, except, I didn't scratch G.J. like I did Darryl. G.J. was my *first* love.

I was afraid of getting pregnant and it was my **greatest fear.**

He wanted sex *all* the time, but I didn't want to because I was not on birth control pills and we didn't use protection.
I pulled back and he wasn't happy. I started rationing my body to keep from getting pregnant.

"Pleaseeeeeeee, Tammmmmy, I'll give up sex just to have yours. Pleaseeeeeee," he begged.

One thing about G.J., he was blunt and outspoken and would tell you what he was thinking. He didn't hold back, and at the time when he told me that, I was too naive and immature to ask him what he meant by that comment, **"I'll give up sex just to have yours**." Who were you having sex with is what I should have asked him. But I didn't.
It seemed like the more I gave, the more he wanted and begged for it. The more I gave, the more he became obsessed. He was getting crazier and crazier.

He wanted to be around me *all* the time. He'd pick me up from work late at night to come with him.
He'd come get me the minute I'd get home.

One night, we opened the back gate to his mom's house. He and his brother lived on the side house that was connected to the main home where his mother lived.

As soon as he opened the gate, the back-porch light popped on. G.J. held my hand as we walked and turned towards the light.

"Nu, unnnnn, I don't know where you think you are going with that little *skank*. You are not bringing her here," G.J.'s mother said.

We didn't say *one* word in response. He held my hand tight as we turned around to walk back to his car.

We were in his car listening to the radio in silence. We didn't say *one* word about what his mother said.

He held my hand and kept rubbing it. I let him, but, I thought to myself, "What the hell is a *skank*?"

I never in my life heard that word before. Is skank the same thing as a whore?

I didn't know her and she didn't know me to call me a skank. Whatever it meant, I knew it wasn't good. I was no skank or whore. I was hurt and upset, but more hurt than mad. Not only was I hurt, but I was nowhere near a whore or skank.

I was a sweet, innocent, intelligent, beautiful young girl in love with *her* son while trying to find my way out of the ghetto. She couldn't keep him away from me and I think that was the problem, and the reason I was *her* definition of a skank.

His mama wanted me gone for some *unknown* reason.

G.J. and I continued seeing each other despite his mother's disapproval, but he took me to his uncle's house the next time we got together.

It wasn't long after the skank incident that G.J. and I pulled up to his mother's home and he grabbed my hand and told me that he was taking me to meet his *mother*.

What? Meet YOUR mother? The lady that called me a *skank* without knowing me? I thought to myself. Her calling me a skank cut *real* deep. I was petrified.

"No, I'm scared. Remember what happened? She doesn't like me."

"Come on, I'm taking you to meet her," he insisted and grabbed my hand while walking into the house towards his mom's room.

My heart was beating out of my chest. I was afraid. I didn't want to be called another skank.

"Please, G.J. don't. Please, let's go. I don't want to meet her," I pleaded.

He wouldn't let go of my hand and proceeded towards his mom room like he didn't hear me.

"Pleaseeeeee G.J., I don't want to goooo. I'm scared," I confessed.

He held onto my hand and took me back to his room.

He was disappointed because he wanted to formally introduce me to his beloved mother who he loved *very* much, but I was scared and I didn't want her to call me another skank. I still didn't know what it meant, and I was not trying to find out.

I didn't meet his mother that night but I have a feeling that she knew more about me than I knew about her. After the night she called me a skank, I never had any more issues going to his house. I assumed he talked to her about me. He knew I wasn't a *skank* and wanted his mother to know that I was *his* good girl.

𝄞 𝄞 𝄞

G.J. loved washing his cars. He always kept his cars neat and clean. He kept my car clean, too and it always shined. He was very meticulous when it came to washing cars. I learned to wash my car from him. He would clean the inside and outside to get every bit of dirt. I mean, our cars were **clean**.

He would drop me off at work to detail my car, but he would take off my stickers, "T.C." I had on my car, and I'd get irritated. He didn't like my initials on *my* car. I'd let him take them off because he was the only one that could keep my car *clean*.

𝄞 𝄞 𝄞

We are at the Car Wash on W.W.White Rd next to Frank's Barbeque and our routine was that I'd hold the sprayer while he scrubbed the car with the sponge.

We got out the car and G.J. goes to the coin machine to get change for the car wash.

I held the sprayer while I waited for him to return.

On his way back, he stopped and talked to a guy that he knew, and while he was talking, a guy walked up to me and started talking to me like he knew me and took the sprayer out of my hand so that he could wash G.J.'s car. He thought it was my car and wanted to wash it for me.

G.J. saw us and walked up to the guy and yanked the sprayer out of his hand.

"OOh man, she's with you? I'm sorry man, I didn't know she was with you. I'm sorry man." The guy apologized religiously; over and over, again.

"Yeah, she's with me." G.J. hissed.

The guy left *immediately*.

G.J. told me to get in the car. He washed his green Chrysler Thunderbird and stared into the car at me the entire time, until we left. He didn't vacuum, he was so mad.

We argued all night and into the next day about this guy that I didn't know. He swore that I knew the dude and if not, then why was he willing to wash the got damn car!

This was the *most* that he and I ever argued.

The next day, I drove to G.J.'s house to pick him up, and we argued over the same incident. It was unbelievable.

I was tired and I told him to get out of my car that I was not hearing it today.

He wouldn't get out my car, so I pulled over and tried to pull him out of my car.

I was under 115 pounds and I know that I couldn't get him out my car but that wasn't going to stop me.

I was boxing him like I was Muhammad Ali. He was bobbing and weaving trying to stop me. He *never* hit me. He grabbed me and threw me over his shoulder like a rag doll. He spun me around until I was dizzy but he got dizzy, too.

Gary pulled up beside us to see what we were doing.

G.J. was embarrassed and tried to pretend like we were not arguing and that we were *playing* around.

"See what you've done? He's going to go back and tell my sister. Just drive. Let's go."

I drove but I still wanted him out of my car. I was *tired* of his jealousy and I wanted to get him out of my car, bad.

His jealousy was driving me *insane* and I had enough. We were arguing about someone that I didn't know. It was ridiculous. I loved only his crazy ass but he didn't understand.

He told me to drive and he would get out. Why did I fall for that lie?
I would drive a few blocks and tell him to get out, but he wouldn't.
I wanted to go home and get away from him.

I pulled into Lincoln swimming pool parking lot across from the East Terrace projects and we were still arguing.

G.J. took my purse and pulled out my wallet and took my drivers' license.

"Give me my damn license!" I couldn't believe he took my license.
I recently received my license and was proud to attain them and he knew that my license meant a great deal of accomplishment to me. I was proud to have a driver's license and he also knew that I was afraid to drive without it.

He held onto my license that was stamped with a big red font that read, "UNDER 21."

"G.J., I ain't playing with you. Give me my license so that I can leave. I'm done with your ass *for real* this time."

"Sit back and shut up. You ain't going nowhere and it's never over between us. You hear me."

"Give me my license before I call the police."
He still refused. I got out of the car and tried to flag down a car to call the police.
I don't know how the police showed up on the scene, if I called them or someone else did, but by the time they got there, G.J. left and hid in the field.
I hid my purse under my car seat and told the police that G.J. stole my purse.

The police went searching in the field and found him. G.J. kept saying that he didn't have my purse or anything that belonged to me. The police searched him, but did not find my license.
I later found that he hid my license inside his sock at the bottom of his shoe.

I left at the request of the police and G.J. walked wherever he was going, I don't know where he went. He wasn't with me and he still had my driver's license.

I passed by G.J.'s house a few days later and saw him outside washing his car. He saw my car and flagged me down. I turned around to see what he wanted. He went inside his house and came back outside to give me my license.
I thanked him and left.

He only gave me my license because he missed me and wanted back in.
I relented and went back to him. But why? Because I *loved* him.

𝄞 𝄞 𝄞

A few days later, we were back together in *his* room.
"G.J. quit. Damn, is that all you think about is sex?"
"I'm not on birth control and I don't want to get pregnant."
"I'm going to be careful so you are not gonna get pregnant," he assured me.
"How? You got a condom?"
"No, I don't need one."
"Go to sleep." I was tired and wasn't trying to have a baby. I wanted out of the courts and pregnancy was not on my agenda. I knew that if I kept having unprotected sex, pregnancy was a possibility.

He kept insisting and I knew it was going to be a long night if I didn't oblige. It would only take about five minutes I thought to myself, and then he'll fall asleep and leave me alone.
Give it to him so that he could be quiet was my mindset whenever he'd start.
I became a master at whatever I *thought* I was doing.
Make him go to sleep was my goal.
It worked each time.
I was G.J.'s NyQuil. I would knock him smooth out and he would fall asleep like a newborn baby.

𝄞 𝄞 𝄞

Our relationship was going well and we were all lovey dovey. I would listen to Stephanie Mills "I Never Knew Love Like This Before" in my car, and when I'd go to G.J.'s house, he'd tell me to bring the cassette in his room so that I could listen to it. He would sing along, too. I didn't know he knew the song, but he did. He was a huge Cameo fan and would sing "Candy" to me all the time, and Gregory Abbott's song, "Shake You Down," and Keith Sweat's, "Right and A Wrong Way." I hated that song with a passion because G.J. would sing, "You may be young, but you're ready, ready to learn" I wasn't ready. He would tease me all the time with that song. Uggrrhhhh, I would roll my eyes and push him away.

It was time for G.J. to finally and formally meet my mother. But before I took him to meet mama, I told my mother to make sure the house was REAL clean and to keep the lights on so that the roaches wouldn't come out to embarrass me.

I can't recall the conversation the day that I brought G.J. to meet mama, but she thought he was handsome. I believe mama knew about him before I took him to meet her because she didn't seem *surprised*. I bet she knew about him since I was seventeen, but never said anything.

One night, G.J. and I was outside *my* house sitting on my car and I sat between his legs. He had officially met mama and he was no longer a *secret*.

I stood up to hug and face him when we heard tires squeal on a car that pulled up in the back of us.
He turned around to see where the noise was coming from, and I see a short, dark-skinned woman jump out of a car and start yelling at G.J.

"Get your ass in the car." She said as she hit him.
He didn't say ONE word, but held his head down, shielding himself from the hits as he got into the car.
I stood there dazed and confused.
What the hell happened? I thought to myself.
I turned around to see if anyone was looking, as I slowly walked upstairs inside the house feeling bewildered.
Why was this lady hitting *my* 'boyfriend?'
Why did he get in the car and leave me here looking dumb?
I was shocked and embarrassed.

🎼 🎼 🎼

A few nights later, my phone rang and I answered.

"Hello, is this Tammy Campbell?" An unfamiliar woman's voice asked.

"Yes, who is this?"

"Bitch, this is Garland's baby mama. And you skinny, bumpy face bitch better stay away from him!"

"Bumpy face? G.J. loves these bumps on my face." I emphasized 'loves' as I clapped back at her. I was insecure about the acne on my face that plagued me throughout high school so when she said, "bumpy face." I knew she either knew me or she had an informant. All these people knew me, but I didn't know them.

"You skinny bumpy face bbbbbb!" She continued to say.
Click! I hung up on her in mid-sentence before she finished the word, "bitch."
Who was she and how did she get my number?
She must have got my phone number from the phone book because mama had the telephone in my name.
She called back and I continued hanging up on her each time I hear her say, "bitch."

She called the next night.

"Tammy, *please* don't hang up," she insisted with a mellow soft voice.
I don't know why I didn't hang up. Maybe it was because her voice was settled and she wasn't calling me out my name or bumpy face.

G.J.'s baby mama, Wendy and I talked that night for the *first* time and we talked many nights after that night. She and I became cool.

She told me that she and Garland were *still* together and that they have a son *and* daughter.
She told me the details of their relationship.
She knew about me from *his* family.
She asked if I did drugs because she doesn't know why G.J. always wants to be around me. She wanted to know what he saw in me.

I told her that I'd never done drugs and G.J. never offered me any drugs. He always said that I was a good girl and he didn't want to ruin me.
She asked why he kept coming back for me.

I didn't quite understand her questions about why he wouldn't leave me alone.
I was a beautiful girl and I didn't need to smoke weed to keep G.J. around me. I was the *opposite* of drugs, and so far away on the other end of the spectrum. I lived in the ghetto, but I never once thought about doing drugs.

She *kept* asking what he saw in me. Why does he want to be around me? I thought it was weird of her to *keep* asking me over and over why he wanted to be around me. She should ask *him*, not me.

She asked if I slept with him, and I said, "Yes." She wanted to know how many times. I didn't want to hurt her so I said, once, maybe twice, but what difference does it make, he was *my* man. I didn't know her, but *knew of* her.

G.J. lied about their relationship.

I told her about the wedding ring that he gave me and how he threatened to take me to Vegas to get married.
She said that she never got a ring. She was upset when she heard about him giving me a wedding ring. In fact, she was the only person besides him and myself that knew about the ring.

She told me that G.J. would take her money to take me places.
I asked why she gave it to him and to stop doing it.

I didn't know how she knew so much about me. She and G.J. had a loyal informant and I hoped he/she got paid well because they were doing a good job keeping tabs on me.

Wendy said the night when G.J. and I were outside and she pulled up on us, he got in the car but as soon as they got to the stop sign at the corner that he jumped out of the car and took off running.
She thought he was running back to me. I told her that I hadn't seen him since that night.

We were comparing notes and she told me other things about G.J. that I'm taking to my grave.

I was shocked and it was totally opposite of the relationship that he and I had.

She told me about the day that G.J. came home with scars on his face and she made the comment, "I see that she kicked your ass."

It was the day that we were fighting about that guy at the carwash, and the day he took my driver's license. She lived close by E.Commerce

Street so it only made sense for him to walk to her house after the altercation between us.

Wendy knew everything about me, but I knew nothing about her. She was very open and honest and didn't hold anything back. She told me *all* her business. I felt sorry for her.

G.J. called a few days later as if nothing happened that night with his baby mama. I decided that it was time to end the relationship for good.

I talked to Wendy frequently over the phone. She told me where she lived and gave me her phone number so that we could hang out.
Lou was young and is only two years older than me. She had G.J.'s first child, a son, at eighteen and his daughter at twenty years old. She loved G.J. more than life and wanted so bad to marry him and be a family.
I didn't blame her. I loved G.J. as well, but not as much as she did.

I felt bad for her and her kids. What he was doing neither of us deserved, especially, the mother of his kids.
I don't know if it was Wendy or me that concocted a plan to catch G.J. in his lies.

I agreed to call her on three-way when he called so that she could listen to our conversation and see that I was telling the truth about him.
I contacted her as soon as he called and I placed him on hold so I could call her. I told her to be quiet when I click over because he's on the other line. I clicked to talk to her after I was done talking to him. I told G.J. to meet me at Walters and Gevers street in a parking lot area. He agreed.

I hung up the phone with him, and Lou and I finished our plan to set him up.
I drove to her house to pick her up. Her younger sister kept the kids.

We drove to the spot I told G.J. to meet me. He stood outside his car eating a burger.

G.J. loved burgers. He probably had me a burger, because there was no way, he would eat a burger without buying me one.

It was dark, but he saw me pull up while Lou hid down in the front seat. He walked to the passenger side of my car and I notified her that he was near, and Lou popped out like the "Jack in the box" toy.

"SURPRISE, you're busted motherfuckerrrrr!"

G.J. was stunned, mad, and shocked. I couldn't tell if he was madder than stunned, but he was pissed.

I set his cheating ass up.

We circled around him like ring around the roses, while Lou yelled all kinds of obscenities at him.

Lou could curse. She cursed like a sailor.

"Fuck you!" he said with frustration.

He took his burger and threw it at her and kicked my car. My car was my baby so that was my cue that it is time to leave and leave him alone.

I *loved* my car.

We left and I took Lou home. Lou and I continued to talk and make plans to hang out together.

We laughed about that night. We talked about the look on G.J.'s face, the burger throwing and the kick to my car.

We set another plan in motion to go to his mama's house to mess up his car since he loved it so much, and he made a foot dent in my car. But our plan failed when we saw G.J. outside washing his car.

We circled around E. Houston Street and the street over, and Lou continued talking shit to him out the window while I drove.

He took the water hose and sprayed it towards her.

We kept circling around him until his mother came outside and shouted, "Lou, get out the car!"

Lou was about to trade places with me and drive, while I hung out the car window to give him a piece of *my* mind when his mother came out.

It was time to go after Ms. Beverly came outside. Lou didn't want to talk to her because she felt that his mother knew about me but pretended like she didn't know.

She felt betrayed by her and thought that G.J.'s mother approved of our relationship or him cheating on her.

I told Lou about the incident of her calling me a skank, but she still didn't believe that she didn't know about me.

Lou and I hung together a few times more before I left to go my way.

G.J. and I saw each other one last time and it was over in my book. He needed to be a father to his kids and a man to his baby mama.

I grew to like Lou and didn't want to partake in hurting her. She was a sweet girl. I didn't want her giving her money to him to spend on me. His kids needed the money.

Lou thought that G.J. and I slept together after that incident because someone said that I was over his house. I was at his house, but nothing happened. It was over between G.J. and me, and I left Lou with **her** man. *Her* baby daddy.

I jumped off the G.J.'s carrousel for good.

Whenever he came around. I told him to go back to his baby mama. When he called me, I told him to call his baby mama. Those were my famous words that hurt him. But I meant it. What he was doing was wrong.

Unfortunately, when I left, it didn't stop G.J. from cheating. I wouldn't say he was a player or had a lot of women because Lou would have told me if it was anyone else besides me. She knew exactly who he was messing with but don't ask me how she knew so much about me.

When G.J. saw Darryl and me together that night, he left without any trouble when I asked him to leave because when he saw Darryl up close, he recognized him, and knew that he worked with his baby mama at Popeye's. He didn't want me to find out about her.

𝄞 𝄞 𝄞

Lou told me that G.J. was dating another girl named, Toy after I left. I often ran into Lou in the streets and we would talk and get caught up on our life.

We never held any animosity towards each other. I didn't hold any towards her. I'm glad she came into my life when she did and saved me from being another pregnant teenager.

She never came after me, but she went after him for cheating. She knew that he lied to me and that I didn't know about her. She understood me and I understood her. We were both in love with the **same man** that broke our *young* hearts.

Chapter 10

The King of Blues

It wasn't long after I swore that I wouldn't have anything to do with G.J. when I met the King of my blues, Mr. Bobby.
I always knew of Bobby because he once tried to holla at me one day when I walked to Steve's store.
I knew of him because of the rumors spread about Bobby and me that G.J. told me about when we were together.

Bobby and my first encounter, he had a long Jheri curl and he wore a lot of different warm up suits. He was always fly.
He was sexy, but I wasn't checking for him at the time because the only man I ever had eyes for was G.J.

G.J. was my heart.

Bobby introduced himself to me one day and asked for my phone number. I didn't give him my number and I told him that I have a boyfriend.
This was the extent of our brief encounter; until, one day he jumped in front of my car as I pulled into the parking space in front of my home. I just got off work.

Bobby was 5'9, medium brown skin complexion, and weighed about 150lbs. He had short hair with waves.

"Hey, I know you. You are Bobby. But didn't you have a Jheri curl? And I haven't seen you in a while," I said.

"Yeah, they made me cut my hair all off when I went to jail. I just got out the joint," he explained like it was no thang.

Why didn't I run as fast as a cheetah when he said that he just got out the joint?
I will tell you why.

When you live in the projects, your self-esteem and self-worth are low to non-existence.

I was too embarrassed to date *respectable* men because of my living environment.

How could I meet a good guy and introduce him to my mom and the project cockroaches all at the same time?

There were no respectable "black" men that wanted to meet a young woman that lived in the Wheatley Courts. The name alone was enough to run them off.

I was stuck dating thugs, jailbirds, and the bottom of the barrel men.

I was a part of the projects.

No good man in his right mind wanted me.

I was considered a project's chick.

My cousin, James was outspoken, and he once told me that my taste in men was in my ass. My taste wasn't in my ass, but it was in my low self-worth.

I was branded, and the odds to fail was stacked way high.

Living in the projects was the blueprint for failure.

It wasn't a matter of how or why, but when you would fall.

Everyone deserves a second chance, I told myself when I heard that Bobby served two years in the state penitentiary.

Bobby was beyond cool. He walked and talked a good game and most definitely he deserved a second chance. I reasoned with myself.

His most unique attribute was that he was humorous.

He kept me laughing in the beginning.

We stood outside my mom's house one day and he cracked jokes on everybody that walked by.

"Look at that little boy with that popcorn hair." I busted out laughing. He had jokes for everybody that walked passed us.

It's funny what men do in the beginning and then flip the light switches on, and all the roaches start scattering.

Bobby was charismatic. He had swag.

He had the ladies, but he didn't have me.

He wanted me.

His resilience got him what he wanted.

🎼 🎼 🎼

We met in 1988, I was nineteen years old. I wasn't a woman, but yet, I was not a girl.

We started dating. He met my mother *before* I introduced him to her.

He *was* bold, Bobby.

My mother would always say, "I saw Bobby, he asked for you."

"You don't even know how he looks mama," I said with a laugh.

"Yes, I do. He sat on the stairs and he has on a red shirt."

Later that night, I met up with Bobby and sure enough, he wore a *red* T-Shirt.

Bobby didn't need an introduction, he let it be known who he was and who he was interested in, Bobbie Jean's favorite daughter, Tammy.

Bobby *loved* the attention. He needed to be seen and loved by the environment around him.

He came from a broken home and grew up in and out of foster homes his entire childhood. He often ran away from the foster homes until he went to live with his grandmother, Maseline in his teen years.

He loved her like a mother, and she was his "Honey Bunny."

She returned the same love for him. But in her eyes, her grandson could do no wrong. It was always someone else's fault, not *her* grandson's.

She spoiled him.

His grandmother didn't live in the Wheatley Courts, she lived a few miles from the projects, but Bobby was always in the courts.

He was out there every day so I guess you could say that he lived there because he fit in with everyone else.

Bobby and I would go to the park and cruise in my car listening to music.

We would hang out at a nightclub called, The 402 located on N. New Braunfels Street.

The 402 was a place where we would go shoot pool, dance, and chill.

One night, Bobby and I decided to go the 402 club to shoot pool and chill.

We parked in the parking lot next to the 402 because there was no parking available at the 402-night club parking lot.

Bobby said that he wanted to stay in the car for a minute and listen to the music and that he would be in the 402 in a little bit; I decided to go inside to shoot pool.

I wasn't inside no more than thirty minutes when Bobby came inside and told me that G.J. was outside and he's tripping with him and that he made him get out the car, and he took the keys out the car ignition.

I was in the middle of my pool game when I stopped and asked Bobby,

"Where the hell is he?"

I walked out the back door of the 402 as G.J. was coming inside.

"What the hell?" I said angrily.

I didn't get a chance to finish my sentence when G.J. picked me up and threw me over his shoulder like a sack of potatoes. He often did this when we were together and it would annoy me.

The patrons stood there and watched, and the only thing you could hear was,

Ooooooohhhhhhhh through the loud thumping music.

"G.J. put me down!"

He said nothing and continued to carry me to the back fence of the 402. G.J. had me pinned up to the fence by the top neck of my blouse in a tight grip.

"What the fuck are you doing with that nigga? You *better* not be doing drugs!" he barked like an angry *man*.

"What? I'm not doing no drugs." I'm shocked that he accused *me* of such a thing.

"What the fuck you doing with him, that nigga is on drugs?"

"G.J. let me go, you are hurting me," I squealed.

"Are you doing drugs? That nigga is on drugs!" he continued to say.

"Nooo, I'm not doing drugs, and he doesn't do drugs."

"Tammy, if I ever catch you doing drugs. I swear before God, I'm going to beat your ass."

He continued his drug rant about Bobby. But why would I believe anything G.J. says when I know he didn't want me with anyone but him? He lived up to his words of me always belonging to him.

"I'm not doing any drugs. Let me go," I continued to beg.

"Get yo car and let's go. I miss you Tammy and I know you miss this," he said, as he pressed his erect penis to my private area.

Only G.J. could go from a drug rant about Bobby into something sexual in a matter of seconds. His multiple personalities would come and go.

"G.J. stop and let me go!"

He slowly let me go, but still had me pinned to the fence and there was no room between us to breathe. His body firmly pressed against mine. We can smell the scent of each other's breath. I know what he wants and what this is all about. He is *always* horny. He's not slick. I thought to myself.

"What the fuck is wrong with you? I'm not with you anymore." I said.

"Who said that? I never ended it. You are going to always belong to me."

"G.J. let me go."

"Nawwww, I'm not letting you go. You are leaving with me."

It was going to be a long night with him so I had to think of something quick to get him to stop. I stopped fighting him and cooperated.

"What about my car?" I asked.

"Get your car and we can drop it off."

"What about Bobby?"

"Fuck him and let him walk!"

"No, that's not right since I brought him here. Give me my keys and I will drop him off at home and then I'll meet you," I lied.

"You better meet me. I miss you, Tammy. I wanna be with you. I miss you," he kept saying.

I don't miss anything. You cheated on me and I have moved on with my life. You have a baby mama and I got a new man is what I wanted to say, but instead, I played it cool so that I can get my keys and get him off me.

"Okay, let me go take him home and I will meet you."

"You better not be lying. Meet me at Walters and Gevers."

"Okay," I agreed.

G.J. gave me my keys and I walked back inside the 402 to get Bobby so that we could leave.

I gave Bobby the keys to the car so that he could drive.

As we left the parking lot, I saw G.J. walking towards my car with a dumbfounded look on his face as I yelled out in front of him and everyone outside the 402,

"I don't want you no more! Leave me the hell alone and go back to your baby mama!"

G.J. walked briskly, slower than a run, but faster than a walk towards my car as Bobby sped away. I thought he would try to kick my car, but we had enough speed that he couldn't reach us in time. He looked as though, he wanted to run after us but decided not to and how embarrassing it would look. He is G.J. and he couldn't let people see him running after my car with *Bobby* driving, and me yelling out to him,

"Go back to your baby mama."

"Mannnnnnn, I thought you said that you are not with G.J. no more?" Bobby said in a nervous tone.

"I'm not."

"Then why the fuck is he tripping like that?"

"I don't know, but he needs to leave me the hell alone and go back to his baby mama."

I assured Bobby that I had nothing to do with G.J. and I don't know why he was tripping. It had been over a month that I was done with him after finding out about his baby mama.

"Well, I'm just saying. That nigga can't be coming up on me like that. I mean, I don't know what you and him had. I'm only going by what you tell me. Nigga shouldn't be acting like that if y'all are through." Bobby said.

I didn't tell Bobby what G.J. said about him being on drugs because I didn't know if he was lying or not. Why would I believe *him*?

I spent too much time that night trying to explain the situation between G.J. and me. There was no us! We were done, but with the way he acted that night, it seemed like I was lying and trying to get Bobby caught in the crossfire. A love triangle.

I was so mad at G.J. I was *tired* of him trying to sabotage my relationships. He didn't want me, he couldn't stand to see me with nobody else. If he wanted me, he wouldn't have left me when I was seventeen and he wouldn't have lied and cheated.

I was tired of him tracking me down. I was tired of his informants. I didn't know who his informants were or how he knew where I was, but he did. As much as I loved him, I wanted him to go back to his baby mama and be a man and a father to his family. He belonged with them, not me.

I was *cute*, *single*, *young*, *no kids*, and no attachments to anyone. I was a *hot* commodity. I didn't want a man with kids or baby mama drama.
Bobby fit the description of what I wanted at the time. He had *no kids* or baby mamas. I was happy with him. *Temporarily* at least.

I was hurt by G.J. too many times and I wanted to finally move on with my life. I cried my heart out the *first* time he left me but, not this time.
I was not jumping back on that rollercoaster.
I had enough
hurt,
pain,
jealousy,
controlling,
and baby mama drama from him.

It was 1988 and it was *over* between G.J. and me.
He hurt me.
I hurt him.
We hurt each other.

Chapter 11

King Don't Love NOBODY

The first hit should have been the last. It was only the beginning. If I could do it all over again, it would have been the last and I would tell every young girl that if a man ever hits you ONCE, it is time to leave.

"Don't you ever put your hands on me!" Bobby yelled as his hands went upside my head.
We were driving one night along Lamar Street when Bobby hit a big bump in the road. The bump was so deep that it hit the bottom of my car hard. I was crazy about my car and I didn't want anything to happen to it, but I was also generous with my car and I would let others drive it.
"What the hell man. Pull over and let me drive. You are going to tear up my car." I was annoyed with him.
He kept driving and ignored me like he didn't give a damn.
"Stop the car!"
He wouldn't stop the car, so I hit him first and he hit me back. I hit him back and he went upside my head. I went back upside his head even harder.
I told him to get out my car and to walk home, and he did. I drove off and left him there. I was in a state of shock and embarrassed that my boyfriend beat me in my head.
My head hurt.
I got home and saw my mother in the living room and I didn't say a word about the abuse. I was too embarrassed to tell my mother that Bobby beat me in my head. She probably would have shot him.
I had no physical signs of being in an altercation because, he beat me in my head, not my face.
This was the first time besides the slap from Darryl that a man has ever put his hands on me.
I was with G.J., but he never hit me. Darryl never hit me, again after that kick in the testicles incident.

This was all *new* to me. It was not only new, but it was damn right embarrassing.
My boyfriend *hit* me. I was appalled.
     What made it more appalling was that I didn't mimic the words that I never wanted to see him again, like I did when Darryl slapped me.

     What the hell is wrong with me? This is *clearly* a RED flag.
Bobby is an abuser, but I still wanted to be with him.
He didn't apologize about that night.
He never hit me, again. He was sorry, but he did not apologize.

𝄞 𝄞 𝄞

I have never seen anyone like Bobby.
He was fun to be around.
He was entertaining.
He was charming.
He was charismatic.
He was popular.
He lived on the wild side of life.
He was crazy.
I was intrigued by his status in the hood and thuggish stunts.
He had creed.
He had game.
I had none. I was a green grasshopper.
I was with him so that made me have a glorified hood status.
A lot of women wanted him.
But I had him.
He was mine and I was his.
There were no ifs, ands, or buts about it.
There were no kids.
There was no baby mamas or baby mama drama.
It was known that he was my man and I was his woman.
He never asked me to be his woman, but I knew I was when he introduced me to his homeboys. He would call me *his* woman.
     I was nineteen years old and he called me his WOMAN.
     His sister asked him what he was doing with me and called me a little girl. He told her that I was not a *little* girl and that I was nineteen.
     She wanted him with *her* friend that she hung with because her friend had a crush on him. The friend was cute and had a nice body.

I was slim and had a little summ, summ in the rear backside, but nothing like his sister's friend.
She would see us together and roll her eyes at me.
He told me about her, but said, "I don't want her. I want you. Fuck her."
    He was twenty-six years old and he was *my* man.
In my young, immature eyes, I didn't see myself as a "woman." I saw women my mother's age as a "woman." My mother was a WOMAN.

    I had a huge awakening when he called me his WOMAN because it meant that I had to act like a WOMAN.
Bobby let everyone know that I was his WOMAN before I knew.

    One evening, we were at his grandmother's house and the phone rung; he answered it and told the person on the opposite line not to call him anymore because he has a WOMAN.
    He was talking about *me* because I was the only "woman" standing there listening to him hang up the phone.
    I was his woman even before we had sex because we were chilling, but unlike G.J., Bobby never pressured me for sex. EVER.
    He didn't care about sex and never touched me or violated me in any sexual manner.
I loved that about him because we could hang out *all* night and sex was never mentioned.
    We were dating for about five months and still, the topic of SEX was never discussed.

    Bobby would call me at work because he'd say that he wanted to hear my voice.
    G.J. used to call at times as well, but I'd hang up and tell him not to call me. I would tell my co-workers to monitor my calls. If it was Bobby then give me the phone, if it was G.J. then tell him that I wasn't here.
It was weird how the tables turned.
I had fallen for Bobby and I was over G.J.

    The first time Bobby said that he loved me, he called me at work and told me.

He didn't need sex to tell me that he loved me. Unlike, G.J., he *pondered* his love for me because,
"How could he be in love if we never had sex?" G.J. called it infatuation, not love. G.J. said that he was 'crazy about me' but Bobby said his feelings for me, was LOVE.
I was elated because he said that he *loved* me.
He wasn't infatuated or hung up on sex, he loved *me.*
Bobby was up front with his feelings for me.
He didn't beat around the bush. He said it, and meant it, and make no mistake about it.
He wanted to be around me day and night. We were *always* together.
He held my hand in the clubs and was very protective.

Women would call out his name and he'd whisper to me,
"These hoes in here calling my name because I'm with my WOMAN. Fuck them hoes."
There he goes, calling me his WOMAN, again.
He'd ignore them like he didn't hear them and it was all about *me*.
Bobby Brown was very popular during this time and people often called Bobby,
Bobby Brown.
He *loved* it. He would be the only guy in the club with sunglasses on at night.
He always wore sunglasses for some odd reason.
His entire demeanor excited me *at the time.*

𝄞 𝄞 𝄞

It was five months or more into our relationship before Bobby and I were intimate.
It was the first time that I ever enjoyed sex.
Bobby was gentle, careful, patient, and had a nice stroke.
I was not experienced but I knew that being with him was *different* than when I was with G.J.
There was no pressure.
No threats.
No begging.
It was pure, come as you are, I will *wait* until you are ready type of acceptance.
He won me over with his *patience.*

I wanted more of him.
It was like our bodies were made for each other.
It scared me, so I went to get on birth control pills because being with him was addicting and scary, and I didn't want to get pregnant.
He was a smooth operator.
We wanted to spend more time together.
We went around looking for an apartment to move in together. One apartment complex off Southcross, the rates seemed reasonable, but for some reason, he wanted to skip that apartment complex.
"I hope you are not moving me into an apartment complex where your ex-girlfriends lives," I said.
"Doris lives in the Southcross apartments," he admitted.
Doris was his woman before me. They were together prior to him going to prison.
I was glad that he told me, but I didn't know why we wasted time driving to the apartments.
We continued searching for apartments in our price range and one that wasn't "ghetto."

𝄞 𝄞 𝄞

It was the beginning of 1989, and my mother was going through a huge depression stage. Her kids were growing up and everyone had moved out, and I was moving out, soon.
She was aware that Bobby and I were looking for an apartment to move in together.
She was not happy and told me one of the greatest and wisest advice that I still follow to this day.
"Tammy, make sure that you can pay your own bills and don't depend on a man's income for your rent."

During this time, my mother and my relationship was up and down.
I spent more time with Bobby and less time with her and she didn't like it.
Bobby was taking away *her* Tammy.
I wanted to be with both, but I loved being around Bobby.
I wanted to wake up and go to bed with him next to me.

My mother would let me sneak Bobby inside my room to spend the night without Alfred knowing, but we were tired of the sneaky visitations.
We wanted to be together.
Our bodies craved each other like crack cocaine and it was the driving force for the reason we wanted our own place.

It was Valentine's Day in 1989, Bobby came to my job to bring me chocolates and the most beautiful card that I'd ever seen.
 I don't know if the card was beautiful because it was from him or the way it was made and what he wrote inside. I still have the card.

 Before I met Bobby, he told me how he was not affectionate and how badly he treated women.
He treated women like dirt; he'd get what he could get, and then leave them.
He often told me how he would leave and make women cry.
He had White, Hispanic, and Black women.
He had one White girl that he called, "Snow."
He was a player and let it be known how he treated women.
Women had a week to give up the nappy dugout or else he was gone.
And when they would give up the nappy dugout, he would still leave them crying.
 I always held this against him in the back of my mind.
I felt remorse for those women. I was one of those women that was left by G.J. for not giving him sex.
I walked in those shoes, and not too long ago.

 Bobby was changing when it came to me.
He was more open about his feelings. His "King don't love nobody" rhetoric changed.
I had Bobby doing things that he had never done with any other woman.
I had him going to the park holding my hand.
He took me to the zoo.
He took me fishing.

One day, we were at his kinfolk's house and I asked him to go fishing, and I told him that I had rod and reels. He said to go get them and we can go fishing.

I went home to get the fishing poles and a short time later, I pulled up to his kinfolk's home with my fishing poles and ready to go fishing.

His kinfolks were on the porch when I drove up.

I heard them laughing as Bobby walked to my car and said,

"I thought you said you had *rod and reels*? These are *bamboo sticks*."

"Yeah, I know. That's what I mean," I didn't see the difference between rod and reels and bamboo sticks. I wanted *him* to take me fishing.

His grandmother was tickled pink and said,

"Gone Bobby and take her fishing and then go to HEB and buy some fish to pretend like you caught them."

They all erupted in laughter.

Bobby got in the car, and said, "Mannnnn, you and these bamboo sticks. I can't believe you did that. Embarrassing me in front of my family."

I'm like, "let's just go. The bamboo sticks can catch fish."

He always laughed about the day I pulled up at his kinfolk's house with my bamboo sticks.

We later got rod and reels and went fishing a lot.

He was not a fisherman and was allergic to the seaweed or something in the rivers and lakes. His eyes would swell each time we'd go fishing. I would want to stay out longer, but we had to leave because his eye would continue to swell and close.

His family noticed the change in him. He was no longer, "King don't love nobody."

He was more like, "King loves Tammy" and there was nothing he could do about it.

He was hooked like a fish caught on *my bamboo stick*.

No other woman had his heart.

I was a nineteen-year-old that had stolen Bobby's heart.

He didn't know what hit him.

Bam!

Chapter 12

Goodbye Blue

🎼

I was nineteen years old on February 19, 1989 when I moved out of the Wheatley Courts.

Three years in the Wheatley Courts was more than enough. I was an adult and I could make my *own* decisions. I was done with the projects. Good-bye Wheatley Courts!

I started a new journey into womanhood.
I didn't know how to cook since my mother didn't allow us in the kitchen while she cooked.

Bobby gave me money to buy food. I bought a whole chicken, hot dogs with buns, cereal, and other items. I forgot to get knives to cut the whole chicken.

We had a twin bed, a television, and our clothes and nothing else when we moved into Springhill apartments located on the Northeast side of San Antonio, Texas. No dishes, utensils, as a matter of fact, we ate from plastic ware.

The rent was $189.00 per month for a one bedroom and bath. The apartment complex was nice and it had three swimming pools. The grounds were well maintained and it wasn't "ghetto." My apartment had *no roaches*.

I was excited about my first apartment with *my* man.

The first night in the apartment since I didn't know how to cook, we ate chili dogs.
Bobby knew that I didn't know how to cook, so he said,
"Baby, these hotdogs showww issss good."
I thought to myself, there wasn't much to boiling hotdogs and warming chili from a can.

My cooking got better as I began to experiment on my own. I taught myself how to cook.

I did most of the cooking and Bobby did 95% of the cleaning and rearranging the apartment furniture once we bought some.

Bobby was a *neat* freak. He cleaned the apartment even if it didn't need cleaning.

It was only him and I that lived there and he cleaned like we had a house full of kids.

He dusted almost every day. The dishes were not allowed to be left in the sink.

We had a dishwasher, but we never used it, and we washed dishes by hand.

The bed had to be made before leaving the apartment.

Incense was lit, and windows were often open for fresh air even though we had central air and heat.

Bobby spoiled me. He *always* ironed my clothes every day and wiped my shoes clean. When he ironed my clothes, he ironed out *every* wrinkle.

Everything was going good in our relationship until one day, Bobby didn't come home.

He came home the next morning.

I was young, but I didn't play the come home the next day game. It was the first time of many times that I put him out. I could put him out because the apartment was in my name only.

I knew that I had to set some guidelines because if not, Bobby would try to run all over me.

I began to see a different side of Bobby after he stayed out all night. He had always drank beer, but when we moved together, the ugly side of how he handled his drinking came to full circle.

I got to know the **real** Bobby.

He'd get drunk and want to fight.

The first fight we had was at his grandmother's house. They would get drunk and argue with each other.

I didn't drink and I have always hated alcohol. I sat and watched the entire family get drunk and start tripping.

One night, they were drinking and I was there with my niece, Argentina. Argentina often stayed with me when I moved into my apartment. As a matter of fact, she was always with me even before I moved into my apartment. She was the first-born niece, and I told Bobby that she was my daughter. I later told him the truth about her being my niece.

Argentina was four years old and she was with me when Bobby started the argument. We got into a physical fight while the family stood there and watched.

I was getting the better of him when he got embarrassed and picked up a brick from his grandmother's yard and threatened to hit me with it.

At that time, his uncle, Tommie stopped him, and my niece and I got into my car and we drove home.

𝄞 𝄞 𝄞

I swore that I was done with him and just when I was done, he'd be at my doorstep the next day or blowing up my phone crying, begging, and saying how sorry he was and that he would never do it, again. He'd always promised to give up drinking until his next drink, and the fights between us continued.

I know you may wonder why stay with a man that is abusive? Men have a way of manipulating women, and I was almost seven years younger than Bobby. He lied about his age when we first met. He told me he was twenty-one, but I looked inside his wallet and saw his ID, and he was twenty-six.

He was streetwise and I was green. He caught me at a pivotal age in my life and manipulating me was like taking candy from a baby doll.

He would beg and cry crocodile tears to get me back, and the sad part was, that it worked. He was a master at begging me back. At times, he'd be on his knees crying and holding onto my leg like a child stopping me from walking away. He was not the tough guy that the streets knew him as.
He was not the Bobby that didn't care about a woman.
He was the opposite of what the streets knew of him.

Bobby would be good for a few weeks, but then he was back at it once he'd start drinking.
He drank and I didn't see how much he drank until we moved in together. He was out of control at times when he would drink. He was a completely different person.

He was someone that I hated when he was drunk, but when he was sober, he was the sweetest man you'd ever know. He had multiple personalities. I loved the sober Bobby but I wanted to kill the drunk, Bobby.

I would put him out and tell him that it was over. He'd call me in the middle of the night when he finished clubbing and drinking, and say,

"I got another woman that's finer than you and she got better pussy than you, too."

"Well, if that's the case, then why aren't you making love to her, instead of, calling me at 3a.m. in the morning?" I'd respond.

"Bitch, I'mma kill youuuu!"

"You think I'm playing, Tammy!"

"Imma blow yo motherfuckin head off, he'd yell into the phone. He was drunk and mad because I wouldn't take him back.
I'd hang up in his face and take the phone off the hook.
He'd always threatened to blow my head off. I didn't take his threats seriously.

𝄞 𝄞 𝄞

My family didn't know about the abusive Bobby until I couldn't hide it anymore.
It was so bad that I had my sister, Terrie's boyfriend telephone number on speed dial so that he could walk across the pathway to tell my mama to come to my house.
The minute he'd start, I'd sneak on the phone and call Horsey and he would tell my mama, and she'd be at my apartment within twenty minutes.

One night, Bobby was drunk and he started taking all the food that he bought out of the freezer; I got on the phone to speed dial my sister's boyfriend, Horsey. My mother, Alfred, my brother, and Horsey showed up to my apartment within twenty minutes.

The minute Bobby saw them, he immediately dropped the food packed inside a pillow case and took off running.

My stepfather, Alfred, who ran like a cheetah took off after him. He caught him and held him there until my mother and I got there.

My mother started beating him with her fist and he stood there with his head down trying to shield her punches. After punching him more than ten times and telling him not to mess with her Tammy, she turned to me and said, "Shit, I'm tired."

Bobby took off running again and Alfred caught him, and that's when Alfred, my brother, and I started beating his ass.
I stopped because he was getting beat bad, but my step-father didn't stop, he continued beating his ass. It got so bad that I had to stop him before he killed Bobby.

I pulled him off Bobby's ass, and said, "that's enough!"
I didn't want my neighbors to call the police, since it seemed like there were police at my apartment at least every two to three months.

Our fights were so often that the apartment management threatened to have me evicted if Bobby was caught on the premises. He was not allowed in the apartment complex because of the constant calls to the police.
I didn't follow the warning, but the fights between us came to a *slight* halt.

Our relationship was off and on, more off than on. It was toxic and dangerous. Dangerous because we didn't belong together, but couldn't stay away for long periods of times.
Bobby was damaged.
He was addicted to the eastside, even though, we moved away from the Wheatley Courts.
He never wanted to leave the streets and brought the streets that I loathed into our Springhill home.

I left the ghetto months ago and vowed to never return, but I was in love with a man that was addicted to the ghetto and he never wanted to leave.
He was addicted to the streets and me, and I was addicted to him.

There were times that I'd be mad at him and he'd grab me, and pull my panties down and put his penis inside me and say, "Is this what you want, huh?" And I'd calm down and our argument was over. His stroke was deadly and he knew it.

Our bodies fit perfect together, like a completed jigsaw puzzle.

We made music without lyrics.
Sweet music that only he and I understood the unspoken words.
We lived in a chaotic unexplainable world.
We were both mentally sick.
 Mentally sick from a disease that was passed down to him and now, it was being transferred to me to pass it along to the next unknown victim.
It was a deadly cursed pattern, and that's not to make excuses for either of our behaviors.

 Our relationship wasn't always bad. We had a lot of fun in between the fights.
Bobby taught me to swim when I was twenty-one years old.
He swam like a fish and could hold his breath underwater for what seemed like hours.
He'd lay me across his arms while I flapped my arms and feet.
 Once I learned the basics of swimming, I no longer needed his assistance to swim, so he would give me a head start as we raced across the pool. I started beating him, so he no longer granted me head starts. I'd still beat him, but barely. He would cheat sometimes and say that he won, I'd swear that I'd win. I became a pretty good above the water swimmer.
 He got his swimming skills from his father, Tack Mayberry, who used to be a lifeguard for many years.
I acquired my swimming skills from him.

 Bobby was also talented in basketball.
We'd often go to the park and he would shoot basketball with the fellas. I sat and watched in admiration cheering for my man.
He had a nice jumper; in fact, he played for Fox Tech but was kicked off the team because he was caught shooting dice.
He loved basketball and would play almost weekly.

 We took walks in the neighborhood in Springhill. We stayed active.
 One night we were doing laundry and walking to the laundromat and you will never guess who we ran into?
The one and only…….. G.J.!

I don't know if it was by coincidence or design that G.J. was dating a girl that lived in the same apartment complex as me.
The girl he was dating was about 5'9 or 5'10 and brown skinned with a nice curvy body.
She was cute and they made a cute couple.
I felt no jealousy since I have moved on from him years ago during this time.

It was a shock, to say the least because I thought I got rid of G.J. as soon as I left the Eastside, but here he was walking in my apartment complex.

Windsor Park Mall Photo booth: Bobby 26, Tammy 19

Bobby and I were startled and whispered to each other,
"Aww, there goes G.J, I hope he doesn't start no shit."
G.J. saw Bobby and me coming his way.
As we approached G.J. and his girlfriend, he stopped dead in his tracks and his girlfriend kept walking, while Bobby and I passed in front of him.

He gave us the look of death and stood there and watched us for what felt like five minutes.

He said *nothing* and neither did Bobby and me. We continued walking in front of him.

It was an awkward moment because the girlfriend didn't stop, she left G.J. there watching Bobby and I. She looked back to see if he was coming, but he stood there and watched us. I watched him, too, in case he tried to be slick.

I don't know if the girlfriend knew what was going on, but Bobby, G.J. and I knew what was up.

Since that night, I would often run into G.J. in my apartment complex.

"Tammy, let me talk to you," he'd say driving in his car while I walked up the sidewalk.

"G.J., please leave me alone. I don't have anything to say to you."

"Just let me take you to get something to eat and then we can talk."

"What is there to talk about? We don't have anything to talk about," I said as I continued to walk.

"Us! We got a lot to talk about. Where are you going? Let me take you."

"G.J., I don't need a ride. Please, just leave me alone." I meant what I said.

G.J. didn't want me and I often told him, but he denied it. He couldn't stand to see me with someone else, especially, Bobby. He lost control over me when I found out about his baby mama.

I was not relenting and was *never* going back to him. I was done with his games. I didn't want to play anymore and he wasn't happy about it. He didn't like being rejected. He knew that he could no longer control me and that I was not the same *young* girl that came running back to him whenever he'd call. I was not at his beckon call, anymore.

He'd drive off fast after he couldn't get me in his car.

Years had passed since G.J. and I had anything to do with each other. I'd moved from the Wheatley Courts, and now, he was dating a girl that lived in the Springhill apartments.

I was paranoid and wondered if my sister, Tina told G.J. my whereabouts. He always knew where I was, but I didn't know how he knew.

He had a nice-looking girlfriend. I had *my* man who he hated. Bobby and G.J. had some type of beef brewing before I came into the picture.

Bobby told me something about G.J.'s sister liked him back in the days, but she was too young for him, and G.J. never liked him since his sister was crushing on him. If I'm not mistaken, I believe he said that G.J.'s mother was crushing on him, too. I don't know.

The rumor that was started about me giving Bobby some head when G.J. and I were together; and now, I moved on with Bobby.

G.J. damn near lost his mind about my decision.

I asked Bobby about the rumor, and if he was the one that started it. He laughed and said he didn't start the rumor. I didn't see anything funny because it was my reputation, and they tried to throw a monkey wrench in G.J. and my relationship. If G.J. and I were intimate at the time, he probably would have believed it, but since we weren't, he knew it was a lie.

Bobby and my relationship put G.J. over the top.
He couldn't handle seeing us together.
If he could have killed Bobby and got away with it, he'd pull the trigger.

I couldn't care less who G.J. was with. I was done with him and his baby mama drama. He was the reason why I would never date a man with kids. EVER.

I saw G.J. randomly in my apartment complex and he continued his same antics.
I asked him, "Don't you have a girlfriend? Why the hell are you harassing me?"
I threatened to tell her if he didn't leave me alone.

I'd tell Bobby about G.J. and his little antics. He'd say that G.J. was a trip that I must have really put it on him, because I had that niggas nose wide open.

Bobby and I talked about how G.J. claimed some of the girls that he dated, but not all of them.

"Those I claim and those I don't" was G.J.'s way of not claiming women.
We'd laugh because he was a trip.

Bobby wondered if G.J. claimed *me*.

"I don't really care if he claims me because I don't have to lie about our relationship.
Too many people knew about it for it to be a lie," I said.
Bobby knew I was not lying because he saw him and his antics too many times since we been together. He believed me.
But it was VERY important to him to know if G.J. *claimed* me. I wasn't sure if he claimed me, but he tried to warn me about Bobby.

It was one of those days where Bobby was starting mess with me so that he could have a reason to go to the eastside. I fried chicken and I left the grease on the stove in case he'd try to start something with me. He was drinking and I knew the night wouldn't end well.

We started arguing and while he was in the room, I slipped into the kitchen to turn the grease on medium to low without it being too high so that he couldn't hear the sizzling of the grease.

He called me *every* name in the book and I had enough.

G.J. or Darryl has never called me out my name. Ever.

Bobby on this day, he acted like he didn't know my name. Tonight, was going to be the night that he'd never put his hands on me. I meant it and I swore to God, it was going to be the **last** time.

I continued arguing with him and stalling until the grease was good and hot.

He became more and more aggressive, and I made sure that he didn't come close to me. He knew that I would start throwing them b's, and his only way to combat my fist was to get me on the ground and choke me.

I couldn't take him being on top of me because I was claustrophobic and he used it against me.

It was his number one go-to strategy. He'd get on top of me and smother and choke me. I would gasp for air.

We were in the room and I told him to call me whatever he wanted, but he better not put his got damn hands on me!

He continued his name calling and I lead him into the kitchen. The name calling got worse and he lunged at me. I moved back and grabbed the handle of the hot chicken grease.

I picked up the skillet and dashed the hot chicken grease all over his chest area.

"OOOOOOahhhhh...Tammyyyyyyyyy, I love youuuuuuuu! It's burning. It's burning!" he wallowed.

I reached into the drawer and grabbed two butcher's knives.

"Don't you come near me, you motherfucker! I swear, if you touch me. I will kill you!" I meant every word.

"Tammyyyyy, it's hottttttt! It's burningggggg. I love youuuuuuuu!"

He began tearing off his shirt like the incredible hulk.
I got scared and saw that he no longer wanted to harm me and needed my help. I put the butcher's knives down and I took him into the bathroom to put him into the bathtub to run cold water on his burn wounds.

"Look what you did," he cried out.

"I'm sorry. You made me do it. I am not going to allow you to put your hands on me anymore, Bobby. I'm sorry." I cried.

"I'm going to go get some butter. Stay in the bathtub and I'll be right back." I panicked.

I went into the kitchen to get a stick of butter and ran back to his side.
I rubbed the butter on his wounds.
I gave him pain medication for the pain.
He continued to confess his love for me. I apologized for what I did.
I didn't mean to do it, but I was *tired* of Bobby's abuse.
I loved him, but I was not going to take it, anymore.
I *snapped*!
I had to put an end to it or else someone would get hurt. That someone wasn't going to be me.
I had a lot to live for and if he couldn't see it then I had to show him.

I put him into the bed and we both were crying.
He was crying about what I did and so was I.
He was crying from the pain. I was crying because he was in pain.
I never intended to hurt him. He knew it.
We laid in bed thinking of ways to tell people what happened to him.
He was going to protect me at all costs.
And he did.

He loved me with his life. I loved him with mine.

He told people that I left the hot grease on the stove after cooking chicken and he accidentally knocked the skillet over and it got all over him.
He hid from his family because he didn't want to explain what happened. He didn't want them mad at me and blamed himself for what I did.

🎼 🎼 🎼

One day, his uncle who was dating a girl that lived in Springhill, saw Bobby walking to the store. He saw the burns and immediately called Bobby's mother.
She came to get him when I was at work. She wanted him away from me.
She cried when she saw her son's body. I didn't blame her because I would do the same.
The same way she felt about her son's condition was the way my mother felt about Bobby abusing me. My mother didn't like it, either.
I told my mother what happened and she too wanted us away from each other. She saw Bobby and felt sorry for him. I explained to her that he would never put his hands on me and that I wasn't going to stand for it. My mother knew that I lost it for me to do something like that.

🎼 🎼 🎼

Bobby stayed the night with his mother, but he came back home the next day.
I nursed his wounds back to normal with an Aloe Vera plant that I got from his Mexican friend's girlfriend. We often went to their home to chill and they knew us and our toxic relationship.
It took about six months to a year before he fully healed from the incident. The scars were no longer visible.

After that incident, Bobby kept his hands to himself.
He'd start mess but, he'd chill and think twice about raising his hand to me.
We were mentally sick.
We could not and would not live without each other, and no one could keep us apart.
No one could ever understand our relationship.

We didn't understand it.
I was spinning out of control being with him.
I was paying a price and playing with fire, literally, not figuratively.
We were in too deep.
Sinking.
Drowning.
Crazy in love with insanity.

Illusions Night Club Tammy 20, Bobby 27

Bobby (28) Tammy(21)
Windsor Park Mall photo booth.

Chapter 13

Myson

My life was at a standstill. I was with a man that didn't want anything in life but the streets. I often talked about going back to school, but I was deterred by Bobby's insecurity.

He would often say that I wanted to go back to school so that I could leave him for a bookworm.
I would say that wasn't true and how I would *never* leave him. I wanted to go back to school to have a *better* life.
I was working two jobs and still was not getting ahead.

I had so much holding me back and the number one reason was, ME. I was putting up with a lot of mess that I didn't have to deal with.
My self-esteem was getting lower and lower being with Bobby.
He would talk about my weight.
He would talk about my cooking.
He would talk about the acne on my face.
He would say how he was the **only** *man that wanted me.* No other man wanted me because I was too skinny.
He would say how all the women that he had in life were fine and I was the *only* woman that wasn't fine.

I told his friend, Chris, some of the things that he would tell me, and Chris would say,
"Tell that nigga to get with them."
Chris lived in Springhill with us and I met Chris through Bobby.
Chris never told me to leave Bobby but he didn't like the way he treated me and often times, he tried to stay out of our toxic relationship.
It was the best thing for people to do because we would fight and then be right back together.

We would break up and then we would be out at the same nightclub and Bobby would see me talking to a guy outside the club, he would pick up a 40-ounce beer bottle and chase the guy away from me.

He was embarrassing, but everyone knew us and they knew who each one belonged to.

A lot of times, different guys would ask me if I was still with Bobby so that they could get a chance to holla at me, but when they saw him starting shit in the club, they knew the answer.

I had a friend named, Roderick that worked with me at Alamo Heights Nursing home. He worked in the kitchen as a cook and I was a certified nurse's aide.

Roderick lived in Springhill too, and he gave me rides home from work when Bobby and I were not on good terms.

Roderick and Bobby knew each other because Bobby worked in the kitchen with Roderick before Bobby was fired from Alamo Heights Nursing home.

I got Bobby the job at Alamo Heights but it came crashing down because neither one of us could nor should have ever worked together.

There were rumors of him flirting with women, and one girl named, Bronda that worked very close to me was rumored to like Bobby, and someone said that she and Bobby were hugged up together.

When I was told about them being hugged up together, Bronda was off work, so I had to wait until she returned to work to confront her. I waited for Bobby's shift to end to confront him.
I could hardly wait until 8p.m. because I was going to beat Bobby's ass on the job.

As soon as he was done cleaning, I was at that kitchen door. I confronted him about what I heard, but of course, he denied it and I didn't believe a word he said. How the hell was he going to make me look bad up at the job that I got him?

He was done arguing with me and he walked away.
I was drinking a bottled coke soda and I was done with it. He wasn't trying to hear anything I said, so he started walking down the hallway to get away from me, so I took the coke bottle and threw it down the hallway trying to hit him with it.
The bottle kept sliding down the hallway and shattered into pieces.

The nurses and CNAs came to see what the noise was and saw that Bobby and I were involved.

I went down the hallway to clean up the glass and walked back to my area where I was working.

Bobby left to go home.

Bronda came to work the next day and I confronted her fat ass about *my* man. She asked who told me that and it was a lie. She said that she was never hugged up with *my* man.

Bronda was a fat chick. She weighed over 250 pounds but she had a cute face. She looked like the comedian, Monique, but she had slanted Asian eyes.

Bobby never had a thing for *fat* chicks, but I was not leaving anything or anyone to chance because he was a *man* that often cheated on me with different women.

Since that day, Bronda and I never talked, again. The mutual friendship that we had was gone by the wayside. I didn't trust her or *my* man.

Bobby was fired from the job because of the bottle incident and I was allowed to stay since I'd been working there longer. I was also a good CNA.

Roderick worked in the kitchen as the Chef during this incident, and he was a former military (Air Force) guy that liked me. He knew that I was with Bobby but it didn't stop him from keeping his distance.

Roderick always told me how crazy Bobby was and how could I be involved with him?

I could never answer that question because I didn't know. I could not explain it.

𝄞 𝄞 𝄞

One night, I was mad at Bobby because he always did things that pissed me off, like coming home late or not at all.

I decided that I was not going to wait around for him. I left to go chill with Roderick.

Roderick and I went to his friend's house and we chilled for a minute.

We went back to his apartment.

Before I left my apartment that night, I called Roderick on the phone to make sure that he was home.

I was in a hurry to leave home and I forgot to dial another number after I contacted him in case Bobby dialed *69 to retrieve the last number dialed.

We were watching the HBO comedy show, laughing and tripping when Roderick's phone rings and he answered and the person hung up. We didn't think anything of it and kept watching T.V. and chilling.
The phone rang again, and Roderick picked up the phone. It was Bobby on the phone.

"I know my woman is over there, Motherfucker. I'm going to beat your ass when I see you," Bobby told Roderick on the phone.

"Who is your woman?"
Bobby said, me because of Roderick's response.

"Man, Tammy ain't over here. I haven't seen your woman."

"Yes, you have because she dialed your number last. So, I know you're lying motherfucker. Watch when I see you, I'mma fuck you up.

I told Roderick to hang up the phone and take it off the hook. He did and we kept chilling talking about what Bobby said and how crazy he was. Bobby confronted Roderick before about me so Roderick was used to his threats. He didn't fear Bobby.

We continued to chill with the phone off the hook.

I got home later that night and Bobby was up waiting for me as soon as I walked in the door.
He was in the living room watching television lying on the couch.
I took a shower and got in my bed.

I heard Bobby on the phone talking to someone, but I didn't know who.

"Yeah, I know you were with my woman. You motherfucker."

"Huh? What? Oh, this is you, June? Mannnnn, I'm sorry, I dialed *69, I forgot that I dialed your number after I dialed his. This girl got my head all fucked up. I thought I was dialing that nigga, Roderick. Mannnnnn, June, I'm sorry let me let you go back to sleep."

I couldn't help but snicker at that fool. He dialed *his* friend, June's number after talking to Roderick so he could no longer *69 Roderick's number because June's number overwrote it. I laughed.

He was *hotter* than fish grease, but I gave him a dose of his own medicine and he didn't like it.

I never cheated on Bobby but I threatened to. I could never do it no matter what he was outside our home doing. I know that when the day came to leave, there was no turning back and he would lose a *good* woman. There would be a lucky man out there that would appreciate me. I stayed true to my belief and I believed in me.

I was twenty-two years old when I missed my period. I knew I was pregnant even before I officially knew the diagnosis. My period was regular and *never* late. I was on the pill, but I could no longer afford them after three years. The clinics would not supply me free birth control pills.

Planned Parenthood told me that I couldn't get any more birth control pills until I paid my overdue bill. I went to Ella Austin Community center located on Walters street to get pills and they gave me one pack of pills each visit and cut off my supply of pills until I paid my balance.

I had no money to pay for birth control pills, and I was pissed and thought that they should be given away for free.
I couldn't get Bobby to use protection.
I had different colors of condoms Ella Austin gave me to persuade him to use them. He often complained about them being too small.
I didn't know how true it was but they did look cheap and small, but I liked the different colors.
I had red, blue, yellow, and green unused condoms at the bedside.

I waited approximately thirty days until I went to the abortion clinic located on San Pedro Avenue to confirm what I already knew.

I arrived at the clinic to find anti-abortion protesters outside. I ignored them and went inside to get a pregnancy test.

I supplied the clinic with a sample of my urine and waited for them to call me.
I was called and the results were in…

I was pregnant.
I was pregnant with the craziest man on earth's child.
I was not in shock, I didn't want to have a child, especially with *Bobby*.
    Our relationship wasn't healthy and he was no good for me, and he wouldn't be any good for my child.
I didn't want to be tied to him for the rest of my life.

    I acquired information on an abortion and the rates; I told the clinic personnel that I would return when I got the money.
    It was $175.00 and the amount was good for up to eight weeks of pregnancy.
The fee for an abortion doubled after eight weeks, and after fifteen weeks, the clinic could no longer accept me. I would have to go to the hospital to get the abortion.

    I went home thinking how and what I was going to do?
I was cursing out Planned Parenthood and Ella Austin Community center for refusing to give me birth control pills because I didn't have the money.

𝄞 𝄞 𝄞

    I told my mom that I was pregnant and she wasn't upset. I told her that I planned to have an abortion because I don't want a baby with Bobby.
She didn't tell me not to get an abortion, she said that I had to start having kids *someday*.
    I was surprised that my mother said that, I expected her to be in my corner to get an abortion, but she wasn't.
    I told her that I wonder if Alfred could hit me in my stomach real hard so that I could miscarry. She asked if I was crazy that she wouldn't have him do that and the hit could possibly kill me, too.
I didn't know if the hit to the stomach would kill me, but I was willing to take that risk.
    I didn't want a baby with Bobby. He was in and out of jail, and I planned to leave him for good.
    I wanted to go back to school. I didn't want a baby. I was twenty-two years old and felt that I was not mature enough to take care of a child. I could barely take care of me, and to bring a child into Bobby and my madness was not good.

🎼 🎼 🎼

I spent weeks plotting what I was going to do and how I was going to come up with $175 for the abortion.

I hadn't told Bobby that I was pregnant nor told him my plans of having the abortion.

I was at work lifting all types of heaving things; including patients trying to cause a miscarriage.
But to no avail.

The weeks went by and I hadn't come up with the money, and I knew it would be more if I'm past eight weeks of pregnancy.

I finally got the money and I was on my way to the abortion clinic.
My weeks were calculated and I was told that I was pasted fifteen weeks and that they couldn't perform the abortion. I would have to schedule an appointment at the University hospital.

🎼 🎼 🎼

I scheduled the appointment at the University hospital and they advised me that I had to take counseling to make sure that it was what I wanted to do.
I was told that after the abortion, I could get FREE twelve months of birth control pills or get the Norplant. The Norplant is four tiny clear straw looking implants that are placed on the inside of your arm to prevent pregnancy.

I was given pamphlets and information about abortions and I was finally scheduled to have the procedure.

My conscious was bugging out about the abortion. It seemed like every commercial on T.V. was about babies.
I didn't want an abortion. I cried because I didn't want to kill my baby. God knows, I didn't, but I couldn't have a baby with Bobby. It was not going to happen. I planned my exit from him. I didn't want to be tied to him for the rest of my life.

I thought the *right* thing to do was tell Bobby about *his* child before aborting it behind his back. It would be horrible doing it behind his back without his knowledge of having a say in his child's life.
It is *his* child, too.

I decided I was going to tell him. I was not going to wait any longer because the next week was the procedure.

I went to the store to get him a beer and cooked some chicken. I waited late into the night while we were lying in bed watching television.
I told Bobby that I have something to tell him, and he said, "What?"

"Ummmm, I'm scared to tell you."

"What is it? Just tell me."

"Okay, let me whisper it in your ear," I said acting like a silly little girl.
I sat up so that my lips could reach his ear and I whispered…

"Ummmmm, ummmm, the clinic wouldn't give me any more birth control pills and now I'm pregnant. But I don't want any kids so I'm going to have an abortion."
He looks at me and was like….

"What? You're pregnant?"

"Yeah, but I'm going to have an abortion."

"Shiiiiiiiiid, no you ain't! I want my baby! I want my baby!" He was excited and serious at the same time. It was not the reaction I expected. I got out the abortion pamphlets and told him when my appointment was to have the abortion. He looked at the pamphlets and hit them and said,

"Shiiiiiidddddd, you ain't killing my baby! You can throw that shit in the trash because I want my baby! I want my baby! I will kill you, Tammy if you kill my baby. I want my baby! As much as I love kids, you gotta be crazy. I want my baby!"

Bobby loved kids. My sister, Terrie would bring her daughter, Meoshia to the apartment and let us keep her, and he would bathe her in the sink before bed. He always wanted me to call Terrie to see if she wanted us to babysit Meoshia.

He lifted my gown to look at my stomach to see if it was true. I was a little over four months pregnant so there wasn't much to see. He was feeling on my stomach saying how his baby was going to be a boy, and he was going to name him after him. How he was going to dress him with the same clothes as him.

He couldn't wait for his little man.
He threw those pamphlets in the trash along with my appointment date. He didn't want to hear anything about killing *his* child. He planned for his son. Even though, we didn't know the sex of the child. He kept saying, *it was a boy.*

After that night, it was the end of abortion talks. I was having Bobby's child.
It was official and we were not turning back.
Oh my God. Help me.

Bobby told whoever would listen about his unborn son. One girl that lived in the same apartment complex with us named, Kathy, her nickname was Kat; she thought the baby was born already the way he talked about his son. Everything that came out of his mouth was about his son. I told him on several occasions that we don't know the sex of the baby, we would have to find out later. According to him, *he knows it's a boy.*

He was preparing to be a father, well, the best that he knew how. He did a complete change after I told him that I was pregnant.

One of the changes was, we stopped arguing. It was good to live in the home without him coming home late or us arguing and fighting. I thought to myself, wow, our relationship was better ever since I told him that I was pregnant.
Why couldn't it be like this always?

I wore my regular clothes because I wasn't sure if I was going to keep the baby so if I bought maternity clothes, it would be a waste of money. Since we decided to keep the baby, my clothes were becoming too small as the days passed.

One night, after getting off work, Bobby came home with some brand new maternity clothes for me to wear. He said that he went shopping on his lunch break at a shopping store near his job. I can't recall the name of the department store, but what he bought was *cute*.

I couldn't believe he got my size down to the letter, "T."
I thought someone else like a woman picked the clothes, but he told me that he was the one that picked them.

Bobby wasn't the only one preparing for our first child, my mother was preparing for her grandchild, too.

She would call me or drive to my apartment early on the weekends to go to garage sales and the flea market to look for items for the baby.

She bought a crib from a flea-market located off W.W.White Rd. It was a used brown crib, but it was good and I appreciated all that my mother did for her soon to be grandchild.

She also bought me a green suitcase to keep my clothes in when I go into the hospital.
I packed the suitcase with the baby and my clothes.
I still own the suitcase today.

My mother was always buying items for my unborn child. It wasn't until I was six months pregnant when I was informed that the baby was going to be a boy.

Tina recommended that I get prenatal care since many doctors wouldn't deliver the child unless you have prenatal care.
She also knew that Bobby was out there and she didn't want me to catch a disease and transmit it to my unborn son.

Bobby and I had beepers, and the code that I was in labor was "911." It meant that I was at the Baptist hospital in labor and to call and come to the hospital.
We practiced the protocol the further along I got in my pregnancy.
We took nightly walks.
We took a Lamaze class at the Baptist hospital.

During my pregnancy, my mother became more and more depressed.

The doctor prescribed medicine that made her worse.
She was admitted into an asylum and I would visit her every chance I got, which was often.

Life took a toll on my precious mother. She would hear voices in her head and would have constant headaches. She wore a bandana on her head to help ease the pressure of the headaches.

She came home when she got better, but then would later return to the asylum. Her mental illness was like a rollercoaster. One minute, she was the mom that I'd always known, and the next minute, she was another person inside my mother's body.

My mother wasn't only my mother, she was my *best* friend. We were together *all* the time.

We talked about everything and didn't hide any secrets from each other.

She would always wait for me outside on the porch when I'd visit. She knew the exact time my bus arrived and she'd make sure that she was outside to see me exit the bus.
This was her routine.

Where my mom's apartment was located, she could see the bus and when I got off.
My visits always brought my mother great joy.
We sat on the porch and talked about life.
We spent a lot of time, together.

One thing, I would never do was to borrow money from my mother. No matter how broke I was, borrowing money from my mother was off limits. It was a cardinal sin in my book.
I felt my responsibility was to take care of my mother, not my mother take care of me now that I was a grown woman and I had a man.

I was only twenty-two years old, but I was not my mother's responsibility.

🎼 🎼 🎼

June 1992, my mother was at the asylum and Tina and I was visiting her when I felt a warm liquid run down my legs. It felt as though I was urinating on myself.
I told my mother that I couldn't stop it.

"Gurlllll, your water done broke and you are in labor," mama said.
I'm in labor? I didn't feel any labor pains and I didn't know anything about a water bag breakage.
I went to the restroom to try and stop it and clean myself, but it wouldn't stop.

Tina and I cut our visit with my mother short and were on our way to the hospital.

We kissed mama goodbye and I will never forget the look on her face.

She wanted to go with us, but she wasn't allowed to leave under her condition.
I told her that I would call her as soon as I got settled into the hospital to keep her updated.

Tina and I left and I pulled over to the corner store to put gas in the car.
I gave Tina the instructions to page Bobby. She goes to the pay phone to page Bobby with the code, "911" meaning I was in labor and to come to the hospital.
I drove myself to the hospital because Tina didn't know how to drive. We got to the hospital and I was soak and wet from the amniotic fluid.
Bobby called the hospital and I told him that I was in labor and that we are having the baby and go to the house to get the green suitcase. He got to the hospital soon after, and Tina called her boyfriend, Craig to come pick her up.
I was given a Demerol shot because I started to feel labor pains. I understand not to panic due to the Lamaze class training.
I dozed off to sleep and when I woke up the next morning, the pain was worse.
The nurse checked me to see how much I dilated, and it only took eleven hours before Myson was born.
He was 20 1/2 inches long and weighed 7lbs and ¼ ounce.
Bobby cut the umbilical cord while I looked at my son in disbelief.
I couldn't believe I was a *mother*.
Bobby Jr. was born with jaundice and he had to stay under a purple ultraviolet ray light.
We were sad to see our baby in the nursery, the only child under the light.
The doctor said that the jaundice was probably due to Bobby Sr. and my blood types, and that our son's liver wasn't fully developed.
The doctor talked about our son staying in the hospital but I would be released.
I was distraught. There was no way that I was leaving the hospital without my baby.

I checked into my room and I had a roommate that ran her mouth day and night.
She had her baby a few hours before me.
She had no husband and I didn't see anyone visiting her.
She would talk and talk, even though, she saw me with my man.
We wanted privacy, but we had none.

I got up to go to the restroom and Bobby Sr. helped me.
I sat on the toilet and urinated, and big clots of blood came out of me.
The blood clots were as big as mice.
I walked towards Bobby Sr. so that he could assist me when I fainted in his arms.
I called for my mama before I passed out.
I don't know why I fainted, but I lost a lot of blood and my blood pressure was low.
I was worried about my son and how I was not leaving the hospital without my baby.
When I came back to life, I was helped into the bed.
Bobby Sr. was scared because he didn't know what was wrong with me.
I got blood all over his white pants.
I kept telling him that I was not leaving without my baby and that as soon as they bring him to me, to get the car ready and I'm leaving with **MYSON**.
The representative of State Vital records came into my room to get the name of our son.
Bobby Sr. signed the birth certificate and I was ready to go home.

We received good news while we were plotting our escape. The doctor gave orders to release our son, but he needed as much sunlight as possible. She wanted to see him in her office within a week.
We were happy to oblige with the doctor's orders.
We took our baby home.
I knew that my life would make a drastic change.
I didn't know *how* drastic.

Tammy 23, Bobby Sr 29, Bobby Jr. 9 days old. (1992)

Chapter 14

How Do I Say Goodbye To What We Had?

The word got out to G.J. that I had my son. He was aware that I was pregnant and wasn't too happy about it.

He saw my sister, Tina and asked her what I named my son, and she said,

"You know she named him after Bobby."
He asked a question that he didn't want to hear the answer to.
He couldn't stand Bobby.
Darryl couldn't stand Bobby.
Bobby didn't care about G.J. or Darryl because he had what both of them wanted, so he didn't dislike either of them.

Bobby and I often ran into G.J. and when I was alone, he'd still try to talk to me.

The last time I saw him, I asked him, when was it going to end? Meaning, when will he go on with his life and leave me alone. I had gone on with my life, it was long overdue for him to go on with his. I was not going back to him.
No way would I get involved with him.
I learned my lesson to never date a man with a baby mama.
No, meant, no, and I stood my ground. He hurt me too many times and there was no way, I would let him hurt me, again.
He *pushed* me into the arms of Bobby when I tried to escape his pain.

He had a baby mama, and a woman that lived in the same apartment complex as me.
I wanted him to stop bothering me.
I was done with him.
Our relationship ended in 1988.
It was 1992 and we had been over.

On August 28, 1992, I received a phone call from my sister, Tina asking about G.J.'s full name and birthdate.
I gave her the information, and I couldn't believe my ears when she told me that G.J. was found dead in the front yard of a home and it was on the news.
Oh, noooooo, not "My G.J."
I saw G.J. a few weeks ago and I couldn't believe what Tina said. I hung up the phone after talking to her and
I immediately called the funeral homes to see if it was true.
I called Lewis funeral home and they didn't have him.
I called Sutton and Sutton funeral home and they confirmed what I didn't want to hear.

I never saw the news, but from what I heard in the streets was that he was brutally beaten and left for dead.
There were so many rumors surrounding his death that I didn't know what to believe.

Bobby couldn't believe it and he cried when he heard the news. He said that he and G.J. had their beef, but he wouldn't want to see him dead.
I cried for G.J. When I asked him when was it going to end?
I would never want it to end with him losing his life.
I couldn't believe and I couldn't imagine someone brutally hurting *my* G.J.
He was never about that life.
He didn't hang in the streets.
Why would anyone want to hurt him?
I thought about his children.
I thought about Lou and how devastated she would be because, even though, G.J. was with another girl, I knew that she'd always love him.
I hadn't spoken to Lou since 1988.
My son was only two months old and G.J.'s death and my mother's depression were taking a toll on me.

I reflected on our relationship, and his beautiful smile and I didn't know how someone could hurt him.
I thought to myself, maybe if I would have given him another chance, we would have been chilling.

Our last meeting of seeing each other, I asked him when was it going to end?
I felt guilty and bad for the way I rejected him.
Now, that I won't see him around, how do I say goodbye to what we had?
I didn't want to say goodbye, it was too soon to say goodbye.
G.J.'s death was devastating.
It was *officially* over.
But, not the way I envisioned it to be over.

Chapter 15

My Handmade

I had the funeral information to pay my last respect to G.J. I didn't want to go to the funeral alone because I didn't want to deal with G.J.'s mother, in case, she called me another skank.

Shortly after I left G.J. alone in 1988, I was driving down Gabriel Street and Ms. Beverly was outside her mother's home talking with family. She recognized my car and called out to me. She wanted to say something to me, but I had no idea what she wanted. I looked through my rearview mirror and I kept driving. I didn't want any trouble with her. I already moved away from her son, so, I don't know what she wanted with me.

My sister, Tina and our mutual friend, Karen, and I attended G.J.'s funeral. It was packed with family and friends from Fox Tech high school.

I saw Lou and she was distraught. She rode in the family car with G.J.'s family.
I didn't see G.J.'s current girlfriend, I'm not sure if she was allowed to attend.
G.J.'s mother appeared to be the type that wanted to control who he dated and married.
She wanted him to marry the mother of his children, but he never did. Maybe in the near future, he would have settled down and married Lou.

I read G.J.'s obituary and they listed Lou as his wife and even changed her last name to his on the obituary.

Funerals are a show in my humble opinion. I thought this was unfair to the current girlfriend to say that G.J. was married.

He loved his mother and I think he tried to live up to her request but couldn't.

He *loved* Lou, although, he never mentioned it; he only confessed his love for Tracy.

Why he didn't settle down with Lou, I wished I could answer that question. He was young and probably wasn't ready.

🎼 🎼 🎼

I was taking pictures of the funeral. I'm taking pictures of everything, including G.J. in his coffin.

I knew that I wouldn't see him anymore, and I guess I wanted to remember him.

I walked to his coffin and took a quick picture and then kissed him where there were a lot of different lipsticks all over his face from women kissing him.

G.J. was loved by many women.

It was evident by his face. He didn't look like the G.J. that I saw a few weeks before his death.

I thought back to his soft lips; they still looked the same along with his high cheekbones.

I was going to miss his smile.

I was going to miss seeing him around the way.

I already missed the genuine hugs that he used to give me each time he saw me when we were together.

He gave the sweetest and most *genuine hugs*.

After the funeral, my sister, Karen, and I followed the hearse and cars to the cemetery, where I took more pictures.

My friend, Sheila, who dated G.J.'s brother, and has a daughter with him was there and she asked me,

"Tammy, are you here just to take pictures?"

I was taking a lot of pictures and she had a point.

Sheila and I knew each other and hung together when I lived in the Wheatley Courts. My parents knew her cousin's parents and we knew each other from Sutton Homes.

She dated G.J.'s brother prior and during the time I was dating G.J.

G.J. told me to stay out of Sheila and his brother's business because it didn't involve us. I was put into an uncomfortable situation because I was her friend, but dating her baby daddy's brother.

G.J. loved his brother.
He was all about loyalty to his family.

🎼 🎼 🎼

A few months after G.J.'s funeral, Bobby Sr. told me he saw G.J.'s girlfriend at the swimming pool in our apartment complex with a *little ass* bathing suit on.

She was a cute brown-skinned girl with a nice body. I didn't ask him why he was talking to her, I guess it slipped my mind or maybe I didn't care.

"Oh yeah, by the way, G.J. *claimed* you." Bobby Sr. said.
I don't know why it was so important to Bobby for G.J. to *claim* me.
He knew the truth. He was with me when he was tripping. I had no reason to lie about our relationship.

Bobby *needed* to know if G.J. claimed me, though. I don't know how my name got into the conversation between G.J.'s girlfriend and him that day at the pool.
I'm not sure if Bobby asked her or she volunteered the information.
He never said, the only thing that mattered to Bobby was, if G.J. *claimed* me.
If he didn't claim me, was I damaged goods?
I regretted telling him the story of G.J. not claiming certain women and G.J.'s words of, "Those I claim and those I don't."
G.J. was gorgeous and humorous.

🎼 🎼 🎼

Years later, I saw Lou, and we always talked about G.J. She told me that a few days before he was murdered, she was going to leave the guy, she called, Ole boy, and she and G.J. were getting back together.

I told her about him dating the girl in my apartment complex. I don't recall her name, but Lou knew about her.
She knew that I had a son and I'm with Bobby Sr.

I asked her the details of G.J.'s death and she told me. I won't disclose what she told me; it's too personal.

Rest in peace Garland (G.J.).
*I will **always** love you in my own special way.*
April 10, 1965- August 27, 1992.

Life was happening too fast for me. G.J.'s death was surreal. My life as a mother was challenging. My son wouldn't sleep. He had colic and cried day and night, no matter how much gas drops we gave him for his stomach pain.

𝄞 𝄞 𝄞

Bobby Sr. returned to the Bobby before I got pregnant. I knew it wouldn't take long for him to revert back.
He had been holding it in during my pregnancy and the beast had to be unleashed.
The difference was that he had ammunition to use against me this time. And the ammunition was MYSON.

I tried putting him out and moving on with my life, but of course, his favorite saying was…
"You ain't gone keep me away from my son, Tammy. I'll kill you!"
I never tried to keep him away from his son; I wanted to protect my son from his drama.

I explained to him that he could see him whenever he wanted, but it was time for us to end it.
In fact, it was long overdue. My pregnancy was a barrier for what should have taken place *years* ago.
His excuse was, "I want to wake up and go to bed with my son, too."

Every time, we argued, he would get mad and snatch my son out of my arms.
I didn't want to fight over Bobby Jr. because he just got over his jaundice, and he was an infant. He would take my son away because he knew I wouldn't struggle over him.
He would later give him back to me after a little begging and agreeing to take him back.

During this time, he was in and out of his favorite place that he'd visit almost every year, JAIL.
The sad part about his imprisonment was that I was stupidly doing time with him by waiting for his return.

I was dealing with a lot and going through postpartum blues. I loved my son with all my heart but I didn't bond with him until he was about four months old.

He changed my life as far as slowing me down. I couldn't get up and go as I please. I had a little one with me and I couldn't move as fast. I couldn't adapt so I became depressed. The fact that Bobby Jr. didn't sleep through the night was hard to cope.

My cousin, James brought me a baby swing by my apartment, and the only way we could get Bobby Jr. to sleep was to leave him in the swing all night.

I know that's bad parenting, but try not sleeping for days.

🎼 🎼 🎼

I visited my mother and she was a shell of herself.
One day, I went to her apartmnet and we sat on the porch talking. I noticed cut marks on her wrist. I asked her what happened to her wrist? She didn't want to tell me.

"Mama, what happened to your wrist?" I demanded to know.

"You gone be mad if I tell you."

"No, I won't. Tell me what happened to you?" I said with concern.

"Tammy, I tried to kill myself," she said without looking me in the eyes.
My heart dropped and tears rolled down my cheeks.

"Mama, nooooooooooooooooooooooo. Why would you do such a thing?" I asked as I gently examined her wrist.
She said that she doesn't want to live anymore and that all of her kids are grown and could take care of themselves.

"Mama, soooo, I still **need** you. Do you know what that would do to me if you were gone? That would destroy me. Mama, please promise me that you will never do that again?" I begged.
She didn't say anything. She kept her head down.

"Mama, do you hear me? I said with tears in my eyes. Pleaseeeee, mama don't hurt me like thatttttt. Promise me that you won't do that again?"

"Mama, promise meeeeeee!" I kept asking her to promise me but she would not say anything.

"Okay, Tammy I won't," She finally responded.

"I know, but promise me, mama." I wanted to hear her say,

"promise." Because at that time, promise meant that she promised and it was concrete and solid according to the bible.

"*I promise,*" she reluctantly said. I was not convinced but she *promised* me.
I asked her the details of the incident and she told me.
She told me not to tell Tina, Terrie, or Edward and I promised that I wouldn't.

I called her psychiatrist that she was seeing located on E. Commerce Street.
I didn't know what to do. My loyalty was with my mother, but I also didn't want her to hurt herself.

I started spending the night to keep an eye on her. Bobby Jr. and I slept in the living room on the couch.

I was going back and forth to work from her apartment. I caught the bus back to my apartment to drop my son at the daycare and then caught the bus to work.

The raggedy car that I bought for $500 broke down one day when I loaned it to Bobby Sr. to visit his grandmother.

Bobby Sr. was in jail and I was left alone to take care of our son and keep an eye on my mother.

The bus ride was hectic and I was always late to work, so I returned home to my apartment to be at work on time so that I wouldn't get fired.

My mom returned to the asylum a few days later. I would go visit her to keep her company and she would be her normal self.

I barely had bus fare to get to her and she sensed I was broke. Alfred got paid and took her money. I knew this because Alfred always gave my mother his check.

She begged me to take twenty dollars and I kept refusing because my payday was two days away and I could make it.
It was against my will to take money from my mother. I wanted no part of taking money from her.

She convinced me to take the money and unfortunately, I took it. I kept promising that I would pay her back when I got paid.

My mother was released from the asylum and sent home soon after my visit. She told me about another resident trying to rape her. I asked if she reported it and she did but was sent home shortly after.
I called to make sure that it was reported and it was, and they were investigating my mother's allegations.

My mother had a fight with a resident during her previous stay and she told me how big the girl was but it didn't matter because,

"I went round for round and pound for pound with her big ass," my mother said with a laugh.

I laughed too because my mother was humorous with her storytelling. I told my mother I wish I was there, I would have killed that heifer for scratching my mom on her face.

I wanted to say, b*tch but I didn't use profanity in front of my mother.

𝄞 𝄞 𝄞

November 07, 1992, I told my mother that I would be over to bring her the money she loaned me.

I caught the bus after work and noticed when I was on the bus that I didn't see my mother waiting outside on the porch like she **always** did.

I got off the bus and started walking towards her apartment and thought maybe she went inside to use the restroom or maybe she was in the corner of the porch where I couldn't see her.

I walked up the stairs and she wasn't on the porch. The front door was closed and locked.

I have a key to her apartment so I unlocked the door and went inside.

I looked in all the rooms and she wasn't home.

I looked out back where she parked her car and I thought, maybe she took my grandmother to see her sister, Dora Dee?

She knew I was coming over. Where is she?

I walked to the corner bar to use the pay phone and dialed my grandmother's telephone number but she didn't answer.

I saw Tuter and asked her if she has seen my mama and that I'm looking for her.

I walked to my sister's house to see if she was over there.

I waited a little bit longer for my mother because I had to get back to my side of town to pick up my son from daycare. The daycare charged one dollar per minute in late fees picking up a child.

If over an hour late then the police were called and child protective services.

I was tired and frustrated that I couldn't find my mother and no one was home to ask about her whereabouts.

I caught the long bus ride home and picked up my son.

My son and I walked home which was about a ten-minute walk from the daycare center to the apartments.

I got home and put my mother's twenty dollars that I owed her in a bible because it was not to be touched and I would try again tomorrow to repay her.

Bobby Jr. was four and a half months old. I took off his clothes and gave him a bath.

We were settling in for the evening when I received a phone call from Tina.

I answered the phone and Tina was crying.

I didn't ask what was wrong when she blurted out,

"Tammy, mama is deaddddd! She jumped from the bridge and killed herself!"

"What?????" I thought Tina was playing.

She continued to cry and I knew it was real.

She said that she and Craig would be there to get me and my son.

I hung up the phone and my words would never describe how devastated I was.

I screamed and cried **loud**.

I never knew that I could feel so much pain.

Noooooooooo, nooooot myyyyyy mammmma!

I can't live without my mammaaaa….

I sobbed like a baby.

I started cursing out God!

I was throwing punches in the air trying to kick God's ass!!!

"Fuckkkk youuuuuu! You bastardddd!!! How could you take away my mama from meeee?!!!"

"I fuckinggggg hateeee youuuuuu!"

"You motherfuckerrrrr. I knew you were jealous of me and my mama because I loved her more than youuuuuu!"

"They say that you are a jealous Goddddd!"

"Fuck youuuuuu. I hate youuuuuu!" I screamed.

I sobbed and wanted to kill God!

I ran to the bible to open the page where I put my mother's twenty dollars that I owed her.

"Mamaaaaa, I didn't even get to pay you backkkkkkkkkk!"

"How could you leave when I didn't even pay you backkkkkkk?"

"Mamaaaaa, I got your moneyyyyyyy!" I was yelling to the sky so that she could hear me.
I kept calling for her saying, "Mammmaaaa, I got your moneeeeyyyy!!"
I wanted her to come get her moneyyyy.
I had so many emotions running through me that I had lost my mind.

After, I cursed God out and kicked his ass. I blamed me for taking the twenty dollars and not being able to pay my mother back. I knew I shouldn't have took the twenty dollars.
That's all I kept thinking about was…
"Mamaaaaaa, I got your moneyyyyy!"
I wanted her to have her money.

I gathered myself the best I could to get my son ready because Craig and Tina were on their way to get us.

I got to my sister's apartment in the Wheatley Courts and my uncle, Tommie was there trying to console my baby sister.
My brother was like a zombie. He never cries, not even when my dad passed away. He was in shock.
I was in denial.
"Mama is not dead. She's at the State hospital.
Watch, I'm going to get her on the phone, right now."
My sisters kept telling me that she is, but I'm not hearing them.
I picked up the phone to call my mama at the asylum.
"Hello," the person answered.
"Yes, may I please speak to Barbara Campbell?"
"Hold please," I was told.
I had hope. "See, mama *is* fine."
"Oh, she's not here," The voice on the line said.
"Are you sure?" I said with tears and a trembling voice.
I didn't wait for a response….
And that's when it happened, I began to throw up like Della in the hospital the night when my father passed away.
I couldn't make it to the bathroom so I threw up in the kitchen.
I couldn't take the news. It was too much to bear.
My uncle, Tommie stayed and talked to us trying to keep his composure. My mother was his heart so I know that he was hurting.

Terrie blamed herself because she was the last person to see mama alive.

My uncle said that we couldn't have stopped my mother and that the only thing we could have done was prolonged her death, but Bobbie Jean was going to find a way.

His words stuck and he was right, even though, I wanted him to be wrong.

𝄞 𝄞 𝄞

It was only a month ago when my mother *promised* me to my face that she wouldn't hurt herself.
My mother broke her promise and she shattered my heart into pieces foreverrrrrrr.
Myyyyy very best friend and mother was goooone.
She PROMISED ME!
She promised me that she wouldn't hurt herself.
She knew what it would do to me but she did it anyway!
I needed and wanted my mama!
I cried like a baby, a small child taken away from my mother, my best friend, my world that I loved for twenty-three years of my life.
Mammmmmmmaaaaaaa, Nooooooooooooo!!!!
My mother unintentionally killed us both with one leap…

My Handmade
You were the chosen one,
My Handmade.
The uninvited demons
talked you silently into
your grave.

It was November 07,
You ended your life and mine's too.
It was rueful and tragic, how you leaped into
death without leaving a clue.

I've sat for years-wondering why
I've cursed the Lord
for that incurable malady
that caused you to suffer and die.

You were my life mama and perpetually
I will lament and humbly cry.
Ohhh Handmade. You left me too abruptly.
You left without mentioning goodbye.
~I love you, mama

Mama and Me (1991)

Left to right:Tina(26), Terrie(19), Tammy(22), and Barbara(46) pic taken 1992.

Chapter 16

The Never-Ending Blues

It seemed like yesterday in 1985 that we were preparing to bury my father, and now, in 1992, it was time to bury my beloved mother and a part of me.

I was a shell of myself and I didn't know if I was coming or going, and the fact of the matter was, I didn't care if I lived or died. I'd much prefer death to take away the pain in my existing soul.

The memories of my mother were haunting and devastating as we cleaned her apartment and donated her clothes.
I confiscated all her pictures, and that was all I wanted for the memories.

A dear friend of the family, Evelyn, also known as Tuter who would babysit my son while I worked, was at the apartment helping clean. Tuter is my sister's sister-in-law, the sister of Carl.
My uncle, Tommie and my cousin, James along with my brother helped load inside Tommie's truck my mother's belongings to donate to local charities.

The days leading to my mother's funeral, I was unable to properly care for my son, so Tuter and her daughter, Rome volunteered to take care of him for a few days or as long as I needed.

It was time for the viewing of my mother and I didn't have enough strength to see her in the casket, so I stayed in my cousin Sharon's car while my sisters and brother viewed my mother's body. My siblings came back to the car and talked about how beautiful and peaceful mama looked.
She was finally at peace at the age of forty-six.
No more headaches.
No more poverty.
No more Wheatley Courts.
No more *Ghetto Blues*.
Mama was home *free*.

My cousin, Sharon tried to encourage me to go see my mother because it was going to be the last time and she didn't want me to have any regrets, but I couldn't. I was still in a state of shock, denial, hurt, and suicidal thoughts.
I wanted to die or should I say, lay to rest the other half of me that was already spiritually deceased.

We drove around the funeral home's block a few times to see if I would change my mind but I didn't. I couldn't and I wasn't ready to say goodbye.

𝄞 𝄞 𝄞

On November 11, 1992, was the day we laid my mother to rest. The worst day of my life.
The church was filled with patrons, family, and friends; some of them I knew, some of them I didn't know, and some of them, I didn't care to know. I've always thought funerals were overrated and for nosey people to be all in your business.

The family sat in the front rows, and to be honest, I couldn't tell you what was said about my mother or what wasn't said.
I had my head down pretty much the entire time crying out my soul. I saw my four-month-old baby boy with Tuter and Rome. I didn't go to check on him. I'm sure I wanted to, but I couldn't, not at the moment. I was too weak and broken.
Bobby Sr. was in jail, and that's not a shock because he was like a revolving door in the jailhouse.

I had no support system and my greatest supporter was lying deceased within ten feet of me, in a pink coffin wearing a beautiful white dress.

The ceremony ended as each row walked to view my mother for the last time. It was time for my row to see my mother and my cries got louder, even though, I was still in control but not out of control. I stood up and that's when my uncle's wife began pulling me back from my mother's coffin. I was trying to get her hands off me so that I could see my mother for the last time.

Everybody was grabbing me trying to keep me away from my mother.

The funeral home representatives closed my mother's casket and we were outside the church when I was trying to get to the hearse to see my mother.

It was all a blur to me and I don't know how I got outside the church, but my cousin Sharon said, "I think she's having a nervous breakdown."

I was not having a nervous breakdown. I wanted to see my mother and my uncle's wife sparked the controversy as if I was trying to pull my mother out of her casket.

I wanted to see my mother, not pull her out of her casket or hurt her in any way.

My family was able to calm me down and we drove to Meadowlawn burial grounds.

I was cursing and pissed at everybody for holding me back from my mother. I told them to keep their blankety, blank hands off me.

I still wanted to see my mother and was being held back. My cousin, Rochelle called out, "Y'all leave her alone so she can see her mama!"

After my cousin said that, I was left alone and walked to say my last goodbye to the love of my life, my beloved mother.

Barbara Jean Campbell.
January 19, 1946 - November 07, 1992.

Chapter 17

Life after Death

After my mother's funeral, we all gathered at my grandmother's home for the Passover.

My cousins, family, and friends were outside laughing, talking, and chilling, having a good time.

I was outside with everyone, but I didn't feel like laughing, so I went inside the house and went into the back room of my grandmother's home and laid in the bed crying, thinking of ways to kill myself.

I could not live without my mother and I didn't want to. I thought about who would take care of my son and I could not think of anyone but me that could give him the proper upbringing that he deserved.

I thought about taking both of our lives. It was cruel and a selfish act, but it was reasonable in my mind.

I cried and cried for my mother, my son, and me. I cried and prayed myself into a deep slumber, but when I woke up, it was strange because I had no more suicidal thoughts.

It was like God said, "No, my child. I will carry you through it all. Put your faith in me."

It wasn't my son or my time to go home.

We had to live without mama.

It was life after death.

𝄞 𝄞 𝄞

I went home with my sister, Tina and picked up my son from Tuter's house. I missed my son and I looked at his sweet innocent face and I knew that I had to get back to normal because my little guy had no one to depend on but *me*. I was scared, afraid, and fragile about the uncertainties of life but stayed strong.

My son and I lived with Tina for over a month after my mother's funeral and then it was time for us to return home alone to our empty apartment. We had furniture, but the emptiness of being alone.

It was after the New Year (1993) that we returned home, to start a new journey in our life without my mother.

I isolated my son and me from the world, even my family. I didn't want anything to do with anyone.

I felt that my son and I were all that we had and there was no one else.
Myson and me against the world.

I played the ultimate warrior role and the protector of my son. I was never the victim and I never let myself play the victim role. I never wanted to be seen as *weak*; even though, I was withering inside.

I protected my son with my life because if something were to happen to him, it would push me over the edge that I was already hanging over and holding on with one hand.

I was barely standing and hanging on, and whoever lied and said, "Time healed all wounds" was full of it.
The loss of my mother *never* fell under that myth.
I was mad at the world.
I never recovered from mama's unexpected death.
I learned to cope,shield, and play an acting role to perfection.
I survived through the mask that I wore on my face, and I took it off each night to place on again the next day.
I kept the mask, dusted, polished, and fresh to continue its believability.
I fooled many people.
I mourned my mother daily and pretended as though she was still alive, but away, but I couldn't get to her at the time.
I lived this denial for over a year and a few months after her passing.

I was ready to come face to face with reality in March of 1994, so I drove to the Meadowlawn cemetery to visit my mother's gravesite for the *first* time since her death.
I had to face reality.
As unfair as it may have seemed trying to come to terms with my mom's death, I was still not ready, and never will be.
I took my mother's death hard and everyone around me paid the price.

I took my mother killing herself out on the family because my mother wasn't here to take it out on her. I was *angry* and *broken*.

🎼 🎼 🎼

I continued to distance myself from people, but I didn't distance myself from the one man that I needed to get far away from and he was my son's father.

In fact, my life with Bobby Sr. was so crazy and unexplainable that I married him in 1995.

You read correctly. I didn't want to raise my son around another man, and I always wanted him to be raised by his **biological** parents. I also didn't want kids by another man and wanted all my kids to have the same father.

I looked at my life and what I was going through with my daddy issues and I promised not to have my kids go through the same.

This was a huge mistake, because Bobby Sr. was going to always be that street hood guy, and he wasn't going to amount to anything in life. I knew this but, he had a stranglehold on me.

He continued going to jail throughout the marriage and he didn't change. I believed deep down inside that he tried but failed at each attempt.

We went to marriage counseling and I bought into all his broken promises like a fool.

I started distancing myself from Bobby Sr. and went to Legal Aid to file for my divorce one year after the marriage. The paperwork was ready to be signed but he talked me out of it. His crocodile tears won me over, so I didn't go through with the divorce. I gave our marriage and family another chance to work. The more I tried to make it work, the more it didn't, and it was time to plan my escape. I was tired of Bobby Sr. and I had to come to the reality that he was not only no good for me, but he was a bad example around my son.

I was married to him *legally*, but it was never a marriage. It was a marriage by proxy and my baby sister stood in his place. He was married to the prison system and so was I.

Chapter 18

Crossed Paths

I decided that it was time to move on with my life. Although, I was still legally married to Bobby Sr. and the prison system. I started dating. I didn't go looking for men, but they were always around.

It was 1996 and I worked at Grayson Square and Brighton Gardens Rehabilitation home when I met Raphael, a guy born in Nigeria. He was dark skinned, 5'10 or 5'11" and weighed approximately 220 pounds.

I worked two jobs as a medication aide to take care of my son and me. I worked at Grayson Square during the day and I worked at Brighton Gardens part-time administering medications to the elderly during the evening and night shift.

Raphael came to America a few years before we met. He was taking a CNA training course to help his mother that owned a daycare center for the elderly. His mother and father were both in the professional field and came to the country for their education. Raphael's mother was a Registered Nurse and his father was a professor with a PhD.

Raphael was attending school to become a pharmacist.

He saw me one evening as I administered medication and he had to talk to me.

"Hello," he said in his deep Nigerian accent voice.
He was very bold and not shy. He asked for my name and when I responded he noticed the gold tooth in my mouth. He loved my smile, but he was not a fan of my gold tooth, and after our first introduction, he let me know how fond he was of that gold tooth.

Raphael had a pompous attitude and often said,

"I'm only doing this training to help my mother. I'm in school to become a *pharmacist*."

It was nice to *finally* meet a man that was into education. All the men that I met were thugs and probably didn't know what 'education' was beyond a high school diploma.

After our initial encounter, Raphael, instead of doing what he was at Brighton Gardens to do, he followed me around the facility to talk to me.

The instructor of his training class, Wesley had a crush on Raphael. Every time she saw him near me, she would call him to do something. Wesley never deterred him, though, because he continued to follow me around so that he could get to know me better.

§ § §

One evening, I was about to get off work and I received a personal phone call at the Nurses' station. It was Raphael on the phone. His training at my job ended, so he was not able to see me like he did while in training. He offered to pick me up and take me to dinner. I accepted and we made plans the next day. From that day forward, he and I started dating.

Bobby Sr. was in jail, and even though, I was legally married, I considered myself separated and single.

Raphael was aware of Bobby Sr. but we never talked about him. He was focused on living out his American dream and getting to know me, not my husband.

He invited my son and I to his apartment, and that was where we spent most of our time, instead of at my place.

I often asked Raphael what he did for a living and his explanation was that he had his *own* business. He would leave for 'work' early in the morning and leave his car parked at his apartment. Often, I drove his car and parked mine.

He drove a 1996 Toyota Camry and I drove a 1993 Ford Escort standard transmission.

I worked hard for my 1993 Ford Escort. My son and I had an old beat up hooptie that I had to wake up early in the morning to start so that I could get to work on time. I would wake up the entire neighborhood with that car.

One morning, I was taking my son to the daycare center, and the car wouldn't start. My son was three years old, and he mumbled underneath his breath, as he often did,

"Mama, we need a new car." He was right and I was tired of that old hooptie, but it was all that we could afford at that time.

In January 1995, when I received my income tax refund, I took $800 for a down payment to the World Car Center to purchase the Ford Escort.

I liked Raphael's car better because it was bigger with an automatic transmission. I drove his car on the weekends while he was at work.

I kept asking Raphael about his 'own business' until he finally told me the truth.

He took me outside his apartment and pointed to a car and showed me what he did for a living.
I looked at the orange taxi cab and said, "So you are a cab driver?"

He was embarrassed because, you know, he was in America to live his *American dream* not drive a taxi.

I didn't berate him for what he did for a living, but asked why he didn't tell me. I told him that at least it was a *legal* profession.

He was glad to get that secret off his chest. He thought I would leave after finding out that he was a taxi driver. No, I stayed and we planned a trip to go see my favorite team, the Dallas Cowboys.

We were huge cowboys' fans. His siblings lived in Dallas. In fact, he asked his younger brother, Michael to acquire tickets to the game; We went to the game the year Michael Irvin returned from his suspension, when he was caught in the hotel room with the strippers and drugs.

Michael is eleven months younger than Raphael, but his skin complexion is a coco brown compared to Raphael. He was around the same height but maybe fifteen pounds smaller.

Raphael is the oldest of the four children, and he was the caregiver and looked after his siblings.

Michael was the wild child and often lived his life on the edge. Raphael, his sister, Vivian, and youngest sister, Karen, were all the same. They were goal oriented and wanted the *American dream*.

Raphael never planned. He lived life daily and was so unorganized. I didn't know how unorganized he was until we went to

Dallas. I kept asking if his brother bought the tickets and he assured me that everything was taken care of and "DON'T WORRRY," he would reiterate in his Nigerian accent.

When he told me not to worry, I should have worried.

We drove to Irving, Texas and tried to get a decent hotel, but many of the hotel rooms were not available. Raphael paid for a hotel room, but I saw that it looked too ghetto and I was not willing to sleep there; he got his money back and he decided to call his sister to see if we could stay at her apartment.

She said that it was fine, and we stayed the night at his sister's apartment, and that's when I first met his brother, Michael.

Michael was cool and funny. He asked if I had a sister because he thought I was very pretty and wanted to know where Raphael met me.

He and Raphael often spoke in their native language, Igbo and I had no idea what they were saying. They could have been talking about me, but I would never know. They would laugh and Michael would say, "Okay, we have to stop speaking in Igbo, she probably thinks we are talking about her." But they never stopped talking in their native language.

In fact, it was natural to them.

𝄞 𝄞 𝄞

We arrived at the Dallas Cowboys game and our seats were scattered and not together. Remember when he told me not to worry? Yeah, I should have worried. Someone switched seats with us so that we could sit together.

Michael was a few rows below us, and my son, Raphael and I sat together, but my son sat mostly on my lap.

We watched the game, and Dallas won, and we headed home. I was hungry, but Raphael didn't have *any* money, so his brother loaned him money so that he could buy my son and me some Church's Chicken.

I couldn't believe Raphael and how unorganized he was, and how much he lived not only day to day, but more like hour to hour. He didn't have money, but he lived like he did.

During the relationship, there were several eviction notices on his apartment door for failure to pay rent. I would get the notices off the door because my son and I lived there.

I asked him if he needed help paying his rent, but he reluctantly accepted money and offered to pay me back. I worked two jobs and I always saved my money, so I had a little bit of dispensable funds.

Our relationship was going well until another person entered and caused massive havoc.

I already suffered from Bobby Sr. and his infidelity and I was not about to put up with anyone else cheating on me.

𝄞 𝄞 𝄞

Sasha Smith, Raphael's ex-girlfriend was a psycho chick. She attended San Antonio College like Raphael, and she was going to school to become a Registered Nurse (RN).
I knew about her because I found her paycheck stub at Raphael's home one day when I was cleaning, but not only did I find a paycheck stub, I saw a school book that belonged to her, too.

When Sasha found out that Raphael was dating someone else, she made her presence known.

She started calling the house telling me that Raphael was cheating on me with her and how he called her when I was not there, and a bunch of other crazy things.

Raphael and I started arguing about Sasha. He would get on the phone and curse her out but she continued to call and wreak havoc. I was already insecure because Sasha and Raphael were both going to school to get their education, and I had a child and working two dead-end jobs. I envied Sasha, and it made me sick because I had never met or seen her a day in my life.

I don't know if she watched Raphael's apartment, but she knew more about me than I knew about her. Sasha's behavior brought me back to the G.J. and Wendy's debacle with the exception, she nor Raphael had any kids. She had no reason to continue to keep tabs on him or vice versa.

𝄞 𝄞 𝄞

One day, I was passing by my brother's apartment and I saw Raphael's car in the same apartment complex. I knew Sasha lived in the apartments because Raphael told me. I stopped and pulled next to Raphael's car and went looking for him. I was *finally* going to catch him in his lie and beat Sasha and his ass. I was tired of her and him lying to me. I went knocking on random doors asking for Sasha Smith, I was given the correct apartment by one of her neighbor's.

I knocked on Sasha's door like I was the got damn police. "Bam, bam, bam."
The door opens and Raphael was at the door.

"Hi Tammy (he pronounced my name, like "Tommy) I'm glad you are here. Come on in." Raphael said as he stepped to the side so that I could enter the apartment.

I was confused and shocked, and ready to beat some ass, and I was expecting some resistance to get inside. I couldn't believe it was so easy.

The minute I walked in, I saw Sasha take off running into her bathroom. She wore a light pink robe and had rollers in her hair, but I didn't see her face. She was tall, maybe 5'9 or 5'10, she looked like a Godzilla size compared to my small frame.

She ran into the bathroom and Raphael took off running after her. I'm thinking to myself what in the hell is going on here?

Raphael tried to pull her out of the bathroom so that she could tell me face to face what she has been saying about him cheating on me. But she got away from him and locked herself in the bathroom.
She wouldn't come out of the bathroom and kept yelling through the door.
"You see, Tammy. I told you he is cheating on youuuuuuu."
Raphael was mad and kept professing his love for me while she was in the bathroom and wouldn't come out. She kept saying that he was cheating on me.

I asked what he was doing there and he said that she has his apartment key and that she was in his apartment when he wasn't home so he came to get his key.

"Nawww, Tammy, he's lying. He has been calling me. Check my caller id."

"Fine, let's go check her caller id." I have never seen Raphael this upset.

He took me to her phone and we go through her caller id and I see his number, but it was current because he called her about being in his apartment and wanted his key.

I got madder because I didn't know who to believe, so I told her to come out of the bathroom so that we could straighten this out.

She wouldn't. She kept yelling, "See, he's cheating on youuuuu. He's busteddddd."

I kept yelling for her to come out of the bathroom but she wouldn't. I got mad and told Raphael that I was leaving and I don't have time for this shit. He came after me, to explain that he had nothing to do with her and that he wanted his apartment key because she took something out of his apartment.

While Raphael and I got into our cars to leave, Sasha was screaming out of the bathroom window, "Ahhh haaaaa, you are busted. Ahhhh hhaaaaa." She had her face on the window screen. I drove off because I didn't have time for this childish silly ass woman.

She never came out of the bathroom to talk face to face. She yelled the whole time from inside the bathroom and out the window while we were leaving.

You'd think that after this incident, it was the last we'd hear from Sasha, but it wasn't. She continued to sabotage our relationship.

𝄞 𝄞 𝄞

Raphael packed to visit his native country, Nigeria. It was in December 1996 during Christmas time. He visited his country every year so this was *his* tradition.

I bought a Christmas tree and decorated his apartment since my son and I rarely lived at home. The only time we lived at home was when Raphael and I would argue about Sasha. I'd take off to my apartment.

He was visiting his home and I didn't want him to go, because I didn't want to spend Christmas *alone*.

One night, I was going through Raphael luggage that he planned to take home when I noticed a box of condoms in his luggage. He was at work during the time that I discovered the condoms, but when he got home, I asked him about the condoms and he started laughing.
I went smooth off on him. I hit him so hard that he fell on to the bed.

"You leave right now. Get the fuck out of here!" he angrily said.
"I will but not without all the shit that I bought."
I went to the living room and grabbed the Christmas tree and drug it outside and threw it in the parking lot. I was throwing his things and anything that I could find, I was so mad.

I grabbed his Perry Ellis cologne and tried to bust it in the parking lot but, it wouldn't break, the bottle bent, but didn't break. I kept banging it trying to break it but it wouldn't.

I got my son and we left to go home.
I was cursing and promised that I was not dealing with him, anymore.

My son and I spent Christmas alone. I went to buy him another Christmas tree to replace the one that I threw down the street at Raphael's apartment.

The end of the year was near and so was the relationship.

Chapter 19

The Transformation

A few days after tempers calmed the storm, I tried to contact Raphael to apologize for my actions. Each time I called, there was no answer and the answering machine picked up. I knew he wouldn't answer because he was in Nigeria.

Raphael wasn't about that life and I was trying not to be about that life. The life of flight or fight. The life that I was born into and I never wanted to be a part of, *The Ghetto life*.

I don't know why I called Raphael when I knew he would be thousands of miles away.

One day, I decided to call and leave a message and it would be my *last* call if I didn't hear from him. I was in the middle of my message letting him know that I won't be calling again, and to my surprise, he answered the phone.

"Hello, Hello….ummmm, what are you doing home? I thought you are supposed to be in Nigeria?" I asked and was dumbfounded as to why he's answering *his* phone.

"I didn't go anywhere," he said in a low attitudish tone.

"Why not? What about the money you spent on the plane ticket?" I inquired.

He said that he didn't go because of our fight and he would get a refund for the plane ticket. We talked about the argument and he told me that he put the condoms in his luggage to get a reaction from me. He didn't plan to get the reaction that he got, in fact, it was very immature what he did.

Our entire brief encounter was immature. The Sasha Smith incident; the condom incident to name a few. I didn't have time for games.

Raphael and my relationship never recovered from that incident. We continued to see each other but not of the same magnitude as before. Bobby Jr. and I never moved back into his apartment, we remained at home and Raphael would mostly visit us. He needed his space and so did I.

I continued to work both jobs and take care of my son.

𝄞 𝄞 𝄞

I was at work at Brighton Gardens and one of the Licensed Vocational Nurses degraded me in a manner that motivated me, instead of, making me angry.

She said that I am *"just* a medication aide." I was nothing more or nothing less in her eyes.

I was *more* than *just* a medication aide, in fact, I could do her job better than she could, but I didn't have the credentials. I was way more intelligent than she, and I could run rings around her *if* I had the credentials.

Who the hell does this white lady think she is saying that I'm *just* a medication aide?

I was born into poverty, but I was not *dumb*. The only difference between she and I was, that she is white and had the money to further her education, and I didn't.

After her statement, I began to get my life together. I contacted San Antonio College to register for the fall classes. It was exactly ten years that I dropped out of college and I planned my return to school. I had *unfinished* business.

𝄞 𝄞 𝄞

San Antonio College admissions office advised me that I needed to pay in full my defaulted student loan from 1987 before I was eligible to register for classes. I had money saved and I received my income tax check refund, and owed a little over six hundred dollars, so I paid the defaulted loan and registered for the 1997 Fall semester classes at San Antonio College.

I was headed back to school.

I saiddddd, I was headed back to school!

    I told Raphael of my plans to return to school and he was in full support. As a matter of fact, he had been encouraging me to return to school ever since we met. His only advice was, and he often said throughout our *relationship* was,
    "Gold tooth got to go." He was talking about the gold tooth swan cap that I had on my front right tooth.
    I sought a dentist to have the gold tooth removed from my front tooth. I don't know why I let Bobby Sr. talk me into getting such garbage put in my mouth that ruined my smile and front tooth. It was *ghetto garbage*.
My gold tooth was gone.
Earring in my nose was also removed.
I was transforming for the *better*.

🎼 🎼 🎼

    I made plans with both jobs to inform them that I was returning to school to complete my education and I need a change of shifts.
    Co-workers and associates were excited for me, as I was for myself. A nurse at Grayson Square, named, Tammy was responsible for helping me choose my career major.
    She advised me to go to school for computers because it was a lucrative field and would be in demand for a long time, and the pay was good.
    During this time, the computer field was in a frenzy, but in a good way.
    I visited the counselor's office at San Antonio College where I drafted my plan to earn my degree in Information Systems.
I would take the basic courses at San Antonio College and then transfer to the University of Texas at San Antonio to complete my four-year degree. It was known as the 2 + 2 plan.

    My son was five years old and I pledged to him and myself that I would finish school and move to Atlanta, Georgia and I would make a better life for us.
    Raphael and I still saw each other, but like I said before, we needed distance and space. Besides, the Sasha issue and our last

argument played a major role in our much-needed time away from each other.

Bobby's dad was returning home soon and I didn't know how to tell Raphael that I was going back to my **husband**.
I had to try and make my marriage work ONE LAST TIME.

It was weird because the closer it got for Bobby Sr. to return home, Raphael and my relationship started to catch a little more steam.
We were spending a little more time together than before. He was always at my job bringing me roses. He would bring roses often, and Tammy, the nurse would say that he needed to open a florist with the number of roses he brought me.

Raphael was a sweet and kind, gentle man. He was determined to finish his American dream to be a pharmacist.
He was single with no kids. He was a hot commodity. I didn't date men with kids after G.J. so it wasn't unusual that Raphael didn't have kids.
I didn't want *any* baby mama drama and the man that I got involved with had to love my son as much as I love him. I was selfish and I felt that a man with kids wouldn't be able to give my son the same attention that he deserved.
Raphael loved my son like his own. He would take my son to work with him when I was at work, and he'd keep him when needed.

One weekend, it was the last weekend that we spent over Raphael's apartment before I broke the news that we could no longer see each other because my husband was coming home and I was going back to him.
Raphael was hurt and he knew I was making a huge mistake. I knew that I was making a big mistake too, but I at least had to try ONE LAST TIME.

It was on a Sunday and Bobby Jr and I was leaving Raphael's apartment. I packed the things that we had there because we weren't coming back. I gave Raphael a hug and a farewell as he walked us to my car. We were crying, but it was my decision and I felt it was for the best.

I loved Raphael as a friend. He and I would never make it as a couple.

Sasha Smith had a role in my decision to leave Raphael.
The culture difference between Raphael and I played a role as well. He is *Nigerian* and I am an **American Aborigine**.

I love music, deep, soulful R&B music. I am Rhythm &Blues, and I eat, sleep, and breathe it. Raphael had no history of my culture of music. It was a massive knock against him. He knew nothing about singing groups, such as, Earth, Wind, and Fire, The Commodores or The Temptations.

He would never be able to relate to my musical background or culture. We didn't have the same hobbies, such as fishing. He couldn't barbeque. He had no *American* culture.
Dating Raphael was like dating someone of a different race. It was not good.

But the major decision to end the relationship was the fact that I still *loved* my husband. I have always loved him. We had been together since I was nineteen years old. We have a son together. We had history together. We were compatible in every aspect, except, he was damaged and fighting *past* demons from within trying to escape what happened to him in those foster homes when he was a child.

𝄞 𝄞 𝄞

The relationship I had with Raphael taught me a lot. He took us places and we traveled. He was adventurous and spontaneous, and I saw a different world other than the ghetto when I was with him.

He wanted to take my son and me to his homeland, Nigeria but our relationship ended before he got the opportunity. It costed a lot for the plane tickets to Nigeria and he hadn't completed school and I just returned back to San Antonio College.

𝄞 𝄞 𝄞

My first semester of school seemed to fly by. My grades were great and I thought I would struggle with being out of school for ten years.
My husband was home and everything was going well. He came to my school and sat with me before going to work. He helped me with my Music Appreciation course. He did well, helping me in the course. We had fun and he was interested in helping me succeed in school

Bobby loved me, there was no doubt in my mind and it was mutual. Each time, he went to jail, he'd get a new tattoo with Bobby Jr and my name on his body. He has my name on the left side of his chest that was done before our son was born. When our son was born, he got Bobby Jr. and my name tattooed on the right side of his chest. He later got prayer hands with our names on his right arm. He has Tammy N Bobby A/F professionally tattooed in big bold English letters across his back. His back was swollen from the last tattoo. He didn't care, he wanted his back tattooed to show his love.

Bobby Sr(34) Bobby Jr(5) Year 1997

Our relationship wasn't perfect, but nonetheless, every time, he got out of jail, he'll be good for a few months and then he was back to his old ways. The physical abuse had long ago subsided and the reason being was that I fought back and he wasn't trying to deal with the wrath of me.

I missed Raphael, but again, I tried to give my marriage ONE LAST CHANCE.

Raphael was hurt and he asked me to meet him at the Fort Sam Houston Park. I agreed to meet him and that's when he got down on one knee to ask me to marry him. He had tears in his eyes and even though, it hurt me to see him that way, I thought back to Sasha and his childish ways of handling her.

I refused his proposal because I loved Raphael as a *friend*. I loved my husband.

Raphael often came to my job to bring me gifts.

One day, Raphael stopped at my job to bring me a gift. He often came to my job unannounced and when my husband was in jail, it wasn't a big deal so I didn't think anything of it.

I was standing out front in the parking lot of my job talking to Raphael and holding the gift he gave me when I heard someone scream ……

"GET AWAY FROM MY WIFEEEE!"

I looked out the corner of my eyes and saw my husband and son coming down the street. My husband grabbed a big stick out of a yard and started charging up the sidewalk with it.

I immediately ran towards my husband and grabbed him. I told Raphael to get into his car and leave, now!
Raphael was standing there trying to explain to my husband, this madman that he was just *talking* to me.

My husband didn't care what he was doing. He wanted Raphael away from his wifeeee!

I don't know where I got the strength to hold my husband back from kicking Raphael's ass, but it took all of me to stop him. My husband had a look of death on his face. I kept telling him to stop and that he was going to make me lose my job. I think that was the only thing that saved me and possibly Raphael.

I kept screaming for Raphael to leave but he stood there trying to explain. You don't explain anything to a man about his wife.

Finally, my husband came to his senses after Raphael got into his car to leave.

He threw the stick down and told me that he was leaving. He grabbed our son's hand and left.

Even though, the scene didn't look right, it was nothing going on between Raphael and me.

Raphael immediately called me at work and said,

"That's who you are married to? He's crazyyyyyyyyyy! He's trash! That's who you are married to?" he kept repeating.

"Yeah, but you were standing outside of his wife's job talking to her and handing her a gift. Of course, he's going to be crazy." I defended my husband.

I didn't care what was what, Bobby was my husband, not Raphael and you don't talk shit or say nothing about *my* husband. I let Raphael know that I didn't play that and to stay away from my job and hung up the phone.

Nobody, talks about my man. I didn't care what he was, he belonged to *me*.

🎼 🎼 🎼

That night I got home and my husband and son weren't home. I didn't call to look for him or my son. I knew that he would not harm or let anyone harm our son so I wasn't too worried.

What happened earlier at my job looked shady. How could I explain it?

My husband and son came home later that night and he was upset. We didn't talk much about Raphael because he didn't mean anything to me and there wasn't nothing to talk about.

Bobby Sr. didn't forget about Raphael and seemed to randomly visit my job more often.
I knew what he was up to but never said anything.

Our marriage was on its last leg and the Raphael incident opened another excuse for Bobby Sr. to do what he had always done; cheat on me and run the streets.

Bobby Sr. worked at a company called, Clear Visions and he was making decent money. The boss man loved him and talked about how good of a worker he was. He'd take our son to work with him on the weekends because I worked double shifts.

Bobby's co-workers were crazy about our son and thought he was sooooooo cute.
According to Bobby Sr., our son had all the women at Clear Vision. Unfortunately, our son wasn't the only one that the women loved.

𝄞 𝄞 𝄞

It was during Christmas and the company had a gift exchange and one of the gifts that my husband received was a pair of gold playboy earrings.
He thought nothing of the playboy earrings, but immediately when I saw the earrings, I was upset.

"Why would another woman give a married man playboy earring?" I asked.

"Shit, I don't know."

"What you mean, you don't know? You need give them back to her and let her know that you are a married man.

" Mannnn, you're tripping. I'll just pawn them."

"I don't care what you do with them, but you are not wearing them. That's disrespectful to me. You have a wife. I'm not a girlfriend. I'm your wife," I emphasized, WIFE.

I don't know what he did with the earrings. I never saw them in his ear.
The girl that gave him the earrings was Rhonda. She was a tall, dark-skinned woman that wore a lot of gold around her neck, hands, wrist, and of course, a gold tooth.
I didn't have any beef with Rhonda and I don't know if the earrings were a symbol of her trying to tell me something or she thought they were cool in a ghetto way.

Bobby Sr. and I continued to argue about what seemed like everything.

Our marriage wasn't working and he was doing the same things he did that landed him in jail. I said to him that if he goes back to jail *this* time, that Bobby Jr. and I were gone for good. We were moving on with our life.

He kept doing what he wanted to do and it broke my heart to end my marriage.
I had to face reality that it would never work between Bobby Sr. and me.

I called Raphael and cried to him that my marriage wasn't working. Bobby was staying out all night. It was all coming to an end. I'll never forget Raphael's words,

"What are you crying for FOOL? You should be rejoicing, this is the happiest time of your life."

I didn't curse Raphael out for calling me a fool because I was too broken up about my marriage ending, so I let him slide with that 'fool' comment. I was a fool, though.

One night before going to bed, I asked God to take Bobby Sr. out of my life for good.

Two days later I received a call from Bexar County Sheriff's department asking me to accept a collect call from Bobby.
I hung up the phone.
My son and I were moving on…

Tammy (24) Bobby (1) 1993

Chapter 20

Ain't No Stopping Us Now

My marriage was over, but not final. I was still legally married to Bobby Sr. but I called Legal Aid almost each year to ask for a divorce. Each year, I received a "no." I asked if it would be feasible for Bobby to divorce me while in jail because it would only cost five dollars, but according to an attorney, it was best for me to divorce him, instead of, him divorce me. I never asked why and to be honest, I didn't care who divorced whom, I wanted out of the marriage and to move on with my life.

My silence spoke volumes and that's how Bobby Sr. knew it was over. I took our son to see him maybe once and that was it. I stopped responding to his letters, phone calls, and I didn't visit him. Bobby Sr. wasn't the only one that I distanced myself from; I also distanced myself from everyone. I didn't want any type of negativity around me and it was all about my son and me.

Raphael, thought that we were getting back together since Bobby was out of my life, but the ship had sailed. I admired Raphael as a friend.

Raphael would play childish games on AOL, and instant message me as someone else to see how I felt about him. He soon got his answer that we were *just* friends. Friends without benefits. We would hang out together, and he took Bobby Jr. and me to the movies. He would come to my school and tutor me in math and I'd write his English papers. Our friendship was unique, even though, we were no longer in a relationship, we hung out together like we were.

Raphael watched me have a few love interests that weren't serious, and to be honest, I think he was ecstatic that they all ended.

There was always one constant in my life, and it was, Raphael. We were all that we had. I was his only *true* friend and he was mine.

I helped him move from his apartment into his mom's house because he hit a rough patch in his life, so he had to move in with his mother. He later purchased a one-story home located in the North-West side of town not too far from his mother's home.

Raphael, helped me move from Springhill Apartments into Bentwood Apartments on Austin Hwy in March 2000.

I was previously dating a guy named, Walter, an attorney in the military that I met in September of 1999 on AOL.

AOL was a social media website online via the internet. I was thirty years old and he was thirty-nine.

Walter was a traveling attorney, and his ego was as big as California.

He was much older than me and he never married nor had kids. I thought he was a hot commodity at that time until I got to know him. I can understand why he never married or had kids. He didn't have enough room for a wife and his arrogance.

Walter was dark complexed, 5'9 and weighed about 165 pounds, solid build with muscles. He had the most adorable eyes, like the rapper, Tupac Shakur.
He was infatuated with my appearance and body, he often talked about how beautiful I was and how good I looked. I worked out and kept my body in shape. But to be honest, I never really liked men complimenting my looks or body, because there was more to me than my *exterior*.

I was a single mother in school during our brief encounter, and I took my school work *very* serious. I didn't have time to be in a serious committed relationship and I let anyone that I met know that my son, school, and work came first. I was still legally married to my husband. At times, I used marriage as an excuse not to be in a serious committed relationship. I didn't want anything to do with marriage or kids. I planned to finish my education and raise my son.

Walter and I dated for a few months. He asked me to be exclusive in an email. I never confirmed or denied us being exclusive. I assumed that we were, until we got into an argument in February 2000.

It was after Valentine's Day, I called him because neither, he nor I called each other. I was busy with school and I later discovered when I called him, he was busy, too. He wasn't busy with work, like I thought, instead, he was busy with *another* woman.

"Hello," he answered the phone.

"What are you doing?"

"What you mean, what am I doing?"

"Is this a bad time to call? I'm dumbfounded by his pompous attitude towards me and thought he'd be happy to hear my voice. Instead, he told me that he hadn't heard from me in several weeks and that he was dating someone else.

"Whatttttt? Youuuuuuu motherrrfucker! I'm coming over there to kick your ass!"

"Tammy, I haven't heard from you in weeks," he explained.

"I don't give a damnnnnnn. You know my number, you couldn't call me?"

"No, I thought you were with someone else so I moved on," he continued to explain.

"You cheating bastarrddd! I'm coming over there right now and kick your ass!"

"Tammy, don't come over here with that. I haven't heard from you. I thought you moved on, so I met someone."

I slammed down the phone plotting on how I was going to his apartment to kick his ass. The more I plotted, the more my plan fell through. He lived in a gated community and *he* would have to buzz me in to get to him.

I calmed down and thought about my son and my career, and I decided not to go to his apartment. I should be focused on my career, not a man, so I chilled. He wasn't going to take me back to the woman I once was. I tried to get away from the ghetto mentality and I wasn't going to let him take me back.

He called a few nights later to see if I was okay and then that's when he told me about his *new* woman that replaced *me*.

He talked about how she was a *captain* in the military, like him, and how they met at the gym on the military base. And with both of their money put together, how they were going to make all this money and be successful and yada, yada, and a whole bunch of other bullshit that I didn't want to hear, but then again, I did want to hear. I wanted to see how I measured up against her. But the way he described her, I had no chance because I was dealing with low self-esteem.

He made me feel low glorifying a woman that I couldn't compete with. I was a broke single parent college student with two more years to finish my degree.

I listened but I don't know why, he boasted about her like she was the greatest woman that walked on water. The more he talked about her, the lower I sank into despair and hopelessness.

𝄞 𝄞 𝄞

I went to school the next day, and on my way to school, "Please Don't Leave Me This Way" by Thelma Houston played on the radio. My face poured with tears. I could barely drive, my tears were running like a river with broken levees, but I continued driving to school and made it through the day.

I had a few cool friends at school and at work that helped me get over Walter.

My friend at work, Velma told me like it was. She never held back any punches every time I would mention him.

"Ahhhh, Tammy you don't love him. You don't even know what love is. It's just your ego. It's not love."
My friend Tiffany said, "I was in love with being in love."
I remembered her words and wrote a poem about it that went like this…

I'm In Love

What I love or who I choose to love
Is my choice
No one knows what is inside my heart.
You're in love with being in love
Is what they say.
But if it isn't love, and I'm in love
With being in love, then
Leave my lovely thoughts alone.

It is love. I know it is.
The stars in the sky
Will burn and die
The love I have for him is more intense
It will eternally survive.

I'm not in love with being in love.
I know the truth not only by reason
But by the heart,
I'm in love.

Writing *corny* poetry about him was how I got over the heartbreak.

  My friends tried to hook me up with other men, I went out a few times.
  I went out with a guy that I met at the track one day when I was working out. I often ran around the track to keep in shape. I was never fat and I made sure that I wouldn't get fat so I worked out and jogged.
  "Heyyyyy beautiful," he said as I took a break to walk around the track instead of run.
  He worked at the trucking company located next to the track.
He asked to take me to get something to eat. I let him know that I work and go to school and I don't have time for anyone.
He insists that it would only be lunch and nothing else. He gave me his number because I said that I would think about it and I would get back to him.

I talked to my friend, Tiffany and Shelly and they both advised me to go.

I called him and we made plans to meet at a restaurant on W.W.White rd.

It was a FREE meal and what could possibly go wrong?

𝄞 𝄞 𝄞

I commuted to the restaurant immediately after my last class of the day.

He was running a little late, but he called to let me know that he had to pick up his son and had to bring him along. He asked if it is okay. Of course, it wasn't okay. I didn't feel like being bothered with him, let alone his kid.

I was already at the restaurant and I was hungry, so I *pretended* like it was fine.

He arrived with his son, but not only did I meet his son, I met his uncle as well.

I barely knew him, but I had to meet his son and uncle all in one day.

While we were eating, his son was being bad. He kept talking and asking me questions and wouldn't sit still. He kept trying to get the son to behave the entire time while we were eating.

Red flags were flying in the air and I couldn't wait to get out of the restaurant and away from him and his son.

We finished eating and he walked me to my car and asked if he could see me again.

I lied and said, "of course."

He never saw me again after that day and I didn't go run at the same track either, so that I wouldn't see him.

He was too fixated on my appearance anyway to get to know me. He had children and I didn't date men with kids. A lesson learned from experience.

I reported back to Tiffany on how the date went and told her about the son and uncle.

𝄞 𝄞 𝄞

There was another guy that was interested in me named, Lorenzo but he thought he was the shinizzle. The brother was tall, dark, and *handsome*. He *was* fine.

He was attending school to become an attorney. He was a straight "A" student that claimed to not own a television. He spent most of his time at the gym and studying so that he maintained his 4.0 GPA.

I talked to him a few times on the phone, but we didn't have any chemistry.

He was my friend's Tiffany fantasy and I think she wanted to live out her fantasy of sleeping with Lorenzo through me. It wasn't going to happen. I was celibate and I was not thinking of being intimate with anyone. It didn't matter how fine they were.

I was not over Walter, but I moved on because I had no choice; besides, my pride wouldn't let me go back to him.

After a few months passed and Walter and his captain in the military woman didn't work out. He called me for small talk and wanted to know if I still had feelings for him and wanted to reconcile.

He left me for another woman because she had more money and I was a broke single mother.

I wrote about my heartache.

The Puppet On A String

I was gullible and naive
The little puppet on a string.
Catered to your every need
While mine was left incomplete.
 I cried when you left.
I prayed to God for your return
Back into my life.
Willing to sacrifice to make
Our relationship right.
But the harder I tried, the more you strayed
As I faithfully continued to be
The little puppet on a string.
Now, you're back with open arms
And a smile upon your face
Asking for forgiveness and wondering
If my feelings are still the same.
I'm sorry my love, but things have changed
I've moved on to bigger and better things.
So, here's a poem for you and it's
Respectfully written by, what used to be
your puppet on a string.
~May 20, 2000.

Chapter 21

Still I Rise

It was the Spring 2000 semester of school and my love life had taken a nosedive.

But through the adversity of it all, there was one thing that stayed persistent and it was my grades.

I was enrolled in full-time classes and worked double shifts on the weekends at Grayson Square, but I continued to make the Honor Roll.

My pride, my fear of failure, and my son were my motivation. I put all these things and my son as my priority, and anyone that tried to come between my priorities were stopped head on like a car collision. I saw the finish line and I was not letting anything or anyone stand in my way, and that included Walter.

I spoke with him a few times after making my decision to move on. He wanted to rectify his wrong about leaving me for another woman. There was no need to rectify anything. He thought the grass was greener on the other side and I knew that he made a huge mistake by his decision.

I was not over him, but I didn't want him back. I will never ever be another man's first or second choice. If I was not your *only* choice then I wanted nothing to do with them. My G.J.'s experience made my stance loud and clear. I'll share my food, my money, and my clothes, but I will never share my man.

Walter and I remained friends. I know many people can't be friends with ex's but I can remain friends. When you remain friends with your ex, you either never loved them or you are still in love with them. In my case, it was the former, I never loved him. It was my ego that was wounded and misled into an illusion of love.

He lamented about the relationship that he just got out of and he was feeling sorry for himself because he was womanless. I could have kicked him while he was down, but I didn't. I understood the pain that he felt because he inflicted the same pain on me and I wouldn't wish it on my worst enemy. He was not my enemy, so I empathized with his sorrow.

I didn't emphasize enough to take him back. Although, I got over what he did, I could never trust him.

Our relationship was strange from the beginning and it ended strangely. He claimed he never cheated on me and the reason he moved on was that he never heard from me. I never accepted that lame excuse. If he didn't hear from me then he should have called.

I left some personal items at his condo that he wanted me to come and get for months, but I didn't go because I didn't want to see him. My personal items were an excuse to try and see me and get me back, but I declined because I was still hurting. I knew that time would heal my wounds and the tables would turn, and my most powerful ammunition was, *time*.

𝄞 𝄞 𝄞

The school semester ends and once again, I did well in my academics and made the Dean's list. I had all 'A's and one 'B' and that 'B' was in economics. I applied for all types of scholarships and received them because of my excellent grades. I was back in school and excelling.

My son and I attended my awards ceremony to receive my award. I told Walter about my accomplishments, but he never congratulated me.

I was proud of me and what I accomplished. It was my last semester at San Antonio College before I transferred to the University of Texas in San Antonio to finish my degree.

My friends were envious, but admired my willpower.
Tiffany said that she didn't know how I did it because when she tried to work a part-time job and go to school, she didn't have enough time for her studies, and it showed in her grades. I was a single mother, worked full-time, and made the Dean's list. She thought it was amazing.
It was amazing, but at that time, I didn't see how difficult it was or how amazing; I was doing what I needed to do so that my son and I could have a better life. It was commendable, but it was a survival mechanism

that I became accustomed to because you must take what is not handed to you. Life threw a lot at me but I still rose above it all. Still I rise.

🎼 🎼 🎼

It was the summer of 2000 and I was working Monday through Friday from 7am-3pm at Grayson Square until a new medication aide was hired. She was going to school to be a Licensed Vocational Nurse (LVN). Her name was Penny. I didn't care for Penny because she was screwing the owner's grandson who was married.

The company gave her special privileges, so my volatile work schedule was no longer available.

Penny didn't care for me and it was known that we didn't care for each other. There was always respect between us, but she was a lazy medication aide.

After my shift ended, I would mark the bubble pack pills to keep track of the last pill that I gave the patient to make sure that she was giving the patients their medication. I would come back to work the next day and check, and the medication was the same number of pills I left the previous day.

I reported her to the Director of Nurses that she wasn't giving the patients their medications, but it fell on deaf ears. She was sleeping with the boss's grandson. They were aware of her not giving the medication but didn't care about the residences. Their only concern was making sure that they received the residence's checks each month.

During state inspections, if I was not in school, they would call me into work so that I could walk with the state. The D.O.N(Director of Nursing) knew Penny wasn't a good medication aide, and the nursing facility didn't want any deficiencies. I walked with the state inspector each year, and I would pass with flying colors.

I worked for Grayson Square for eleven years and I never acquired a deficiency on the med pass, unlike other medication aides. I was solid when it came to my job, and the reason being was because I cared for the patients as if they were my own flesh and blood.

There was a residence named, Mr. Howard. He was ex-military and he was stubborn as a mule and made our job difficult because he didn't want to take his medication. I found that talking about football made Mr. Howard be more cooperative.

He loved football. He watched football every Sunday. I also loved football and I knew a lot about it. I'd go into his room and start talking football and I'd hit the jackpot getting on his *good* side. I would butter him up so that he would take his medicine.

He began looking forward to me coming into his room to talk football. When I had his attention on football that's when I would sugarcoat him into taking his medicine.

He gave me a huff and gasp type of emotion and grabbed the medicine cup and threw the pills into his mouth. I didn't care what or how he took his medicine as long as he took it. He had a long history of not taking his medication and the nurses made numerous calls to his doctor about his refusal.

Since I found the solution to Mr. Howard taking his medicine, I was sent in his room by the nurses to give his medicine whenever I worked.

I enjoyed talking to Mr. Howard, and our greatest debate was, who was the greatest running back of all time?

"Mr. Howard, Walter Payton is the greatest running back of all time," I'd tell him.

"You don't know nothing. Gayle Sayles is the greatest running back of all time," he'd respond back.

"He didn't even play for a long time. He wasn't the greatest running back. He wasn't as powerful as Walter Payton. Walter Payton broke tackles and carried the defenders on his back." I continued explaining why Walter Payton deserved the greatest running back title.

"You don't know nothing." Mr. Howard would continue to say. He'd say that Jim Brown was better than Walter Payton. I'd lay into him each time I'd come into his room.

Mr. Howard was a prideful man and he'd pretend that he didn't like me because he wanted to keep up that hardcore persona, but deep down inside, he was a teddy bear that looked forward to seeing me on the weekends.

I can go on and on about the residents of Grayson Square, there were many stories and memories.

Chapter 22

Computer Love

𝄞

The computer era was in full effect. The internet was taking the world by storm or should I say, AL Gore's discovery of the internet was taking the world by storm? According to Al Gore, the World Wide Web was *his* discovery. I'd say that Al Gore's invention of the internet goes hand and hand with the Christopher Columbus discovery of America. We all know that there were "Black" Americans in the Americas before Columbus and the Native Americans, and that Black people are the original people of this planet earth, including being first in America.

The internet allowed a connection with people on different continents all over the world; and that's how powerful it was.

𝄞 𝄞 𝄞

I was logged into AOL on July 14, 2000.

AOL was compatible with today's Facebook.

I was logging off and I had just left the poetry chat room sharing a few of my poems when I received an instant message from a person with the screen name, Smuvblkslk.

"Hello, I want the package." The instant message read. Smuvblkslk read my online profile. I thought to myself.

In my profile, I talked about everything that I wanted in a man and life; My profile read, If I were to date a man or if he wanted to take me out to dinner, he would have to make room for three people (my son, me, and my date). I explained how my son meant everything to me and how *we* came as a package. I also talked about how I didn't want a man with stinky feet and how much I liked the basketball player, Malik Rose.

People that read my profile thought it was candid, funny, but honest. It was exactly who I was, my profile was *real talk*. There was nothing fake about me and I made up my mind that I was going to be straightforward with men, and they can take it or hit the door. No exceptions to the rules. If you cheat on me, it was a wrap. If you laid one finger on me, it was a wrap. I was independent. I was not taking no shit from anybody.

My life experiences changed me for the good, and at times, the not so good. The good changes were that I was career and goal oriented. I stopped dating losers or men with criminal backgrounds, drugs, alcoholics, or broken homes.

I didn't date men with kids and that was a big no, no. If you had children, you were automatically excluded.

Life had changed me to be cold at times. If you did anything to offend my son or me, no matter how big or small, I'd kick you to the curb. I was heartless and sensible all at the same time. Every action, there was a reaction, but every mistake I made, I was sincere.

𝄞 𝄞 𝄞

The words continued across my computer screen that read,
"Sorry. I got booted," Mr. Smuvblkslk wrote.
I wrote back with "me too." My screen name was BLoveTK, which stood for Bobby loves Tammy.
"I'm sorry, I'm not Mr. Rose,"
I knew then that Mr.Smuvblkslk either had my profile right in front of him or memorized it.
He knew everything my profile read and it flattered me.
Women love men that pay attention to details and Mr. Smuvblkslk was trending in the right direction. I'd say he was an architect, a bonafide one, if he wasn't, then he should be.

Mr.Smuvblkslk continued to flatter me enough to exchange my photo with him.
I didn't release many photos; I only had one, and it was the picture of my son and me during one of my award ceremonies at San Antonio College.

My husband took the photo of me. I wore a striped blue and white skirt set and I held my award in my hand, with my arm around my son.

Mr. Smuvblkslk liked what he saw in the picture and he sent me a photo.

I was not blown away by Mr. Smuvblkslk look on his face. He looked mean. I asked why he wasn't smiling and that he looked mean.

Throughout the chat, we kept getting disconnected offline, and we kept reconnecting through a slow dialup process that used the home phone landline.

I asked Mr. Smuvblkslk his age,
"Thirty but thirty-one next month."
And he continued the rest of the personal information dialogue without me asking.
"Never married. No kids,"
I responded with "dogs?"
"1" he responded back.
"Girlfriend?" I inquired since he didn't volunteer that information. I anticipated his response and I was elated when he responded with,
"Nope."
"Friends?" I typed. I knew I was being a little too nosy, but these things must be pried out of men because he could be another G.J., where he had a woman but wouldn't claim her.
He typed that he had a few friends but he wanted more from a woman. I asked like what?
"Love."
It took me aback for a minute and I didn't have a good comeback, so I responded with,
"Oh snap."
We chatted a few minutes more before we got disconnected offline, again.
Mr. Smuvblkslk told me to call him.
I asked his name and he typed,
"Emilio. Yes, I'm black," He immediately addressed his race.
I asked Mr. Emilio if his girlfriend would answer the phone when I called, and I received no response. I took that as a "yes."
I waited and waited for him to answer, but silence.
His screen name showed that he is logged off.

Chapter 23

Let's Go Half On A Baby

I stayed focused on my schoolwork and son, but I missed my sisters and brother. I isolated myself from them and thought back to how much fun we had in our twenties. We hung out together a lot in the country and nightclubs.

One night, we were out in the country having a good time. We were shooting pool and cutting a rug on the dance floor. The Campbell children were never shy about dancing and you didn't have to ask any of us twice to cut a rug.

My brother, Edward loved to dance and rap. We would laugh at him all the time because he would dance with the mirror. Meaning, he'd stand by the mirrors look into them to see himself dance.

My brother had a little too much to drink, and we were on the dance floor jamming. My brother was getting off into his dance moves when he decided to try and pick his girlfriend, Tonya up for one of his moves. Tonya said, "Stop James, stop!" She called my brother by his first name.

Tonya weighed about 210 pounds. He always loved big women, especially women with big breast. Tonya had some Dolly Parton's size breast.

"Stop. Stop. Put me down," Tonya continued to yell through the music blasting through the speakers and patrons dancing on the dance floor.

I turned around to see the commotion between my brother and Tonya and that's when I saw him pick her up off her feet for the last time and…….
CRASHHHHHHHH!

The crowd erupted into laughter as Tonya landed on top of the table.

My brother came crashing down on top of her.

"I told you to put me down," she said as she picked herself up off the floor.

My brother was drunk so he wasn't listening, he was having *fun*.

I still don't know to this day what dance move required him to pick Tonya up.

After the crash, we left shortly afterward because Tonya wasn't too happy.

We had good times hanging out. I looked after my siblings, even though, they never knew it.

I was always the designated driver to make sure we got home safe, and I held all drinks so they wouldn't get laced. I didn't drink so I was the watchdog. And if any mess was to pop off at the clubs, we were all there and had each other's back. We were thick as thieves and stuck together. If you talked shit to one of us, you had to fight all of us and that's how we rolled.

We were always close and losing our parents at an early age, we were all the family that we had.

Tammy(25), Edward(27), and Tina(29) (BJ's Night Club) 1995.

I left first to get my mind and life straight because I was tired of doing the same things and not going anywhere in life. I did a complete 180 and took a hiatus for years from my family.

During the time I was missing in action, I met Emilio from Natalia, Texas. Emilio is 5'9" but claimed to be 5'11. A smooth chocolate coco skinned complexion.

After, our initial encounter that night on AOL, Emilio and I talked on the phone until the next morning. I had to be at work the same morning. We connected immediately as if we had known each other for years. I shared a lot of my life story and he did the same. I offered to meet the next day and he accepted the invitation.

Emilio's ideal woman was dark skinned and thick, but I was the opposite of his *ideal* woman. I'm light skinned and was slim to medium in size.
I kept thinking, what if he doesn't find me attractive? He agreed that if we were not attracted to each other then we could be friends because he thought I was *real cool*.

𝄞 𝄞 𝄞

Later that night, it was time to meet Emilio. I suggested that we meet at my job. He agreed to meet me after my shift ended at 11p.m.

I was outside my job when I saw a white dude drive up in a Nissan truck.
I was like, what the hell? I thought he said that he was *black*.
The white dude hops out the truck first to introduce himself.

"Hey, I'm Pate." I looked at him confused.

"Hi, I'm Tammy."

I looked at the truck and that's when I saw Emilio coming from the passenger side to introduce himself.
I had on my scrubs and I felt kind of 'meh' meeting someone for the first time in my work uniform.

Emilio introduced himself and I did the same. We talked for a few minutes and he asked what my plans were for the night.

"I'm going to pick up my son and going to bed."

He asked if I wanted to go with them to get something to eat but I refused.
I was not going anywhere with two men that I just met.

Our conversation brought up my son because Emilio mentioned the *package*. I took my keys out of my purse and showed him a picture of my son and me. He took the keychain and takes my picture out of the keychain picture holder.
I thought he was bold but then again, I liked the bold move.

After that night, Emilio and I talked on the phone *every* day for hours. He mentioned to his friend, Pate, the night we met that I was the *one* and he was going to marry me.

Emilio Age 30 (1999)

Two weeks after meeting, I invited Emilio to my apartment to meet my son.

I prepped my son that I met a guy named, Emilio but his nickname is Nino and that he was coming over to watch movies with us. My son was so excited and ready to meet him.

My son was not a bad child that gave men that I met or dated a difficult time. He was a good kid and wanted a good man for his mother. He also wanted a *daddy.*

𝄞 𝄞 𝄞

Emilio arrived on time, even though, he called a few times because he was lost. I met him downstairs in the parking lot and we walked to my apartment.

I wore black workout booty shorts with a cut off T-shirt because I had just finished working out. I don't know why I didn't take a shower and change clothes.

In fact, my friend Shanita was at my house earlier that day when I had those booty shorts on when I told her that Emilio was coming by tonight.

"Don't you wear those shorts," she said.
I didn't see anything wrong with my shorts. In fact, my body was tight and they look cute snuggling my hips and thighs.
When Emilio arrived, he didn't seem to mind what I was wearing.

Emilio, my son and I watched Rush Hour. My son sat between us. We looked like a family already. My son just turned eight years old. It didn't take him long before he fell asleep and I asked Emilio if he could carry him to his bed. He carried my son and put him into his bunk bed.

We were about to watch another movie, so I bent down to search for a movie, not realizing I had on my booty shorts. I'm sure Emilio didn't shy away from looking at my perfect figure.
I came to my senses and chose any movie so that he could stop looking at my ass.
I never turned around to catch him, but I felt his eyes watching me.

We didn't finish the movie because it was getting late and he had to leave and take his brother's car back to him. His car was getting repaired and in the shop at the time, so he had to borrow his brother's car to come and see me.

I walked Emilio to the car and we stood in the parking lot to talk a little more before he left.

One thing, I loved about Emilio was, the way the street light shined on him as he looked into my eyes.
He had a neatly trimmed goat-tee and he wore a sun visor cap that sat on top of his bald head.
The way he looked at me was so sexy. I knew I would see him again because our chemistry was too strong. Our chemistry had a combination of hydrogen, oxygen, phosphorus, and carbon dioxide. All elements of the periodic table. Our attraction to one another was undeniable fiyah. Smoking hot and deadly. I wanted to find out more about him and his story.

We hugged as our bodies suffocated and entered each other's personal space, but he nor I cared. We enjoyed the moment and didn't want it to end. He had to leave and so did I.

I told him to call me to let me know he made it home safely. I walked up the stairs satisfied and elated with this man that had already embraced my son and me.

🎼 🎼 🎼

Emilio and I were head over heels for each other. If we didn't see each other, we were on the phone every chance we got. My friend, Shanita would accuse me of hiding in the patient's room so that I could talk to Emilio on the phone. She often came down the hallway of Grayson square looking for me, and I'd hide because I wanted privacy to talk to my *man*.

Emilio never asked me to be his woman; oh wait, yes, he did, on the first night we talked on the phone. I jokingly said for him to let me know when we are a couple so that I won't have to assume.
He asked me that night on the phone if I would be his girlfriend. We laughed it off but I knew deep down inside, he was serious.

He never officially asked me other than that night, but from the amount of time and energy we spent together, it was an unwritten official rule that we were together.

He lived forty-five miles or more away from me, and he often traveled to come see my son and me.

As soon as he got off work, he'd call and wait until I invited him over. One day, I asked him why he called first and told him to come to my apartment after work. He came every day, immediately after work after my invitation.

🎼 🎼 🎼

Our relationship was moving fast like a whirlwind. He enjoyed his time with my son and me.

My son sat at the edge of the stairways of the apartment complex and waited for him to arrive so that he could watch him swim at the neighborhood swimming pool. Sometimes, I thought Emilio would come to see my son more than me, that's how much time and attention he gave him. Bobby Jr. considered Emilio *his friend*.

It was a little over five months into our relationship when Emilio started mentioning a child. I was adamant about not getting married or having any more children.

I had gone through a lot in my life and those were the two things I wanted no part of.

When I first met Emilio, I told him that I probably wouldn't make it past my 40th birthday.

I was barely hanging on in life and I held on because of my son. Emilio didn't like to hear me speak that way and assured me that it was going to be all right.

He told me one night,

"Tammy, I know that I don't have a lot to offer you, but one thing I will offer and that is to take care of your son on the weekends while you work. He will be safe in my care and you don't have to worry about him."

My son's babysitter was Tuter, but Bobby Jr. hated staying with Tuter on the weekends. I'm sure he voiced his hatred of Tuter's house to Emilio and could be one of the reasons he offered to take care of him.

Emilio worked Monday through Friday, but was off on weekends. I was in school during the week and worked on the weekends.

Emilio taking care of my son on the weekends took a huge burden off me. I was very thankful to have him take care of him.

He took care of my son as if he was his own biological child.

He was attached to him. They were attached to each other. He was Emilio's shadow.

I was always afraid of my son telling my business, especially, telling my new man my business. Ever since he was young, he had always told my business.

𝄞 𝄞 𝄞

One day, we are at the dentist office getting my son's dental checkup. He was four years old. Bobby Jr. hopped onto the dentist chair to get his X-rays done, and the dental assistant asked,

"Hi, Bobby. How are you doing today?"

"My mama got fleas in her urrrparment," My son mumbled under his breath.

The dental assistant chuckles because she heard what he said but wasn't quite sure, so she asked,

"Whattttt?" in her giggly voice.

"MY MAMA GOT FLEAS IN HER URRRPARTMENT," he said louder.

I must have turned red as an apple I was so embarrassed. I explained to the dental assistant on how we *had* a flea outbreak in our apartment, and then I turned towards my son and said,

"Remember Bobby, we got rid of them a longggggg time ago." Bobby Jr. reached down to scratch one of his legs and said,

"I knowwwww but they still biting me."

The fleas were exterminated by the apartment complex management and were gone a long time ago. I had no idea why he brought up those fleas during his dental checkup.

Bobby Jr. told all my business. Sometimes when we'd go visit people, I'd tell him not to tell mama's business. I didn't know whether to prep him or not, because I didn't want to spark his memory. It was a double edge sword with my son telling my business.

I took good care of him, and he had the best of everything. I worked hard to keep him dressed in the latest air Jordan's shoes and fresh haircuts.

Emilio saw that I was a good mother and decided that I was the *woman* to bore his children. He began dropping hints by walking up behind me and whispering in my ear, "Let's go half on a baby."

That phrase was part of a song recorded by Jagged Edge, a hot R&B group that was very popular during that time.

I'd giggle and say, "You're so crazy."

The more time he spent with my son and me, going half on a baby became more and more *not so crazy, but more of a reality*.

We were both thirty-one years old and we weren't getting any younger. He was a good man that loved my son. I was a good woman that loved my son. We were crazy for each other.

Emilio and I had our ups and downs in our short time being together, but there was something constant about us, I was trying to escape my past and Emilio was trying to escape his present, living in Natalia.

Our escapes were the perfect collision and we collided head-on.

Chapter 24

The Innocent One

Emilio and my relationship was in the beginning stage but we were a couple. He was *my* man and I was no longer on the market. I saw a long-term commitment with him and not a short-term one.

He had a sincere, beautiful heart; a sensitive and a very caring man. Emilio saw the *interior* of me, not my exterior. Unlike, Walter, who was materialistic, pompous, cheap, and rude.

Walter called me one day out of the blue and I told him that I had a new man and I was not trying to hear anything he had to say.

I wanted my things that I left at his condo months ago and I made plans to pick them up.

"Oh, you got a man?" he said.

"Yep, I've moved on with my life. I want my things too, so I will let you know when I will be by to pick them up."

"Oh, who is the nigga?" he inquired.

"Someone that you don't know and it's none of your business," I said matter of factly. I wanted to talk about picking up my things, not *my* man.

"You know I'm going to take you away from that nigga?" he reiterates multiple times during the conversation.
I wished him good luck because he had absolutely no chance in hell to take my *man's* place.
His pompous ego was wounded and he knew deep down inside that he messed up months ago when he left me for *Ms. Captain.*

When Emilio and I first became a couple, I let him know from the beginning that beating and cheating were not allowed in the relationship. If either occurred, then I was gone and there would be no coming back. To this day, I still hold on to my convictions.

Walter lost a good woman and now he was trying his best without doing too much begging to get me back. He claimed he made the biggest mistake of his life and I assured him that he did and now he had to live with it.

I wanted my things from Walter, and I told Emilio that I was going to his apartment to get them.

Emilio at the time, was very insecure because of a previous relationship.
He knew that Walter hurt me but, didn't realize how adamant I was about never having anything to do with a man that cheated on me.

Emilio gave me a lot of flak about going to pick up my things from Walter so I decided against it.

Walter called and asked why I didn't come to get my things, and I told him that my man didn't want me to.
This infuriated him, and his failing words of how he was going to take me from that nigga fell on deaf ears.

It was over and there was never any going back. I told him that he made his choice months ago and it wasn't me. I've made mine and it wasn't him.

I felt good about the table turning on Walter because I knew they would, it was a matter of time, and the time was now. It was over, and he couldn't take what happened back. I no longer wanted him. I wanted Emilio.

Emilio and I continued the *half on a baby* talk. It was a major decision for us to ponder. I was in school and I still had another year to complete before graduation and the struggle of being a single mother was still etched in my mind.

Our relationship was getting deeper and growing more serious. Our time spent together as a family was a reality. My son loved Emilio and the feelings were mutual. We all love each other. He took care of my son on the weekends like he promised. He took care of him even when he and I argued, he'd still come from Natalia to get Bobby Jr. like he was his father and didn't want anyone else taking care of him.

Emilio was his dad in my son's heart and mind. No man has ever spent as much time with Bobby Jr.

He took him fishing, swimming, and played video games with him. He gave him the attention he needed and desperately wanted from a dad.
I thought to myself, if he loves my son in this manner then I'm sure he'd be the same way with his *own* child.

There was only one condition with Emilio to finalize the going half on a baby. He was a religious man and he wanted to get married before having a child.
Married???? I was *still* legally married to Bobby Sr.
Emilio knew it so I didn't understand how or why he was talking *marriage*?
Legal aid would not grant me a divorce and I didn't have any money for one.
I didn't know how much it was to get a divorce.
Emilio offered to pay, but why should he pay for my divorce? I didn't know if he was serious about paying or not, but if he was, it wasn't *his* responsibility.

I accepted the terms of having a child and I promised Emilio that as soon as we have the child then we can get married.
Do you hear how backwards this agreement was? It made sense to us at the time because we were thirty-one years old and felt that we were getting closer to the age of being too old to have children. We both agreed to go for it. Before we agreed to have a child, we were silly and wrote a Constitution.

Emilio thought of things that he wanted from me, and I wrote things that I wanted from him. He only had seven things that he wanted from me, but I wrote things for the present and future, and things that could possibly happen.

We initialed and signed the Constitution and sealed it with our thumbprints.
We were so silly.

I told Emilio that it was easy for me to get pregnant. I planned accordingly and around the times of my fertilization. I got a calendar and made notes of what days I was most fertile.

A few weeks later, my period came and Emilio was disappointed, but I was not, because we started late in the month and we missed the mark.

The next month, I waited and waited for my period. I was always regular and my period came like clockwork each month. A week later, still no period. I waited a few more days and went to buy an over-the-counter pregnancy test.

Emilio was at work during the time I took the test. I kept telling him that I was pregnant, but he was in denial, scared, and didn't think it would happen so *quickly.* He didn't want to get his hopes up high and be disappointed because he wanted a child.

𝄞 𝄞 𝄞

I got a foam cup out of the kitchen and went into my ½ bath bathroom
I opened the pregnancy test and read the instructions. I took the foam cup and peed in it. I sat the cup on the countertop. I examined the urine and didn't see anything unusual. I thought I could tell if I was pregnant by examining my urine. I dipped the pregnancy kit stick into the warm urine, and according to the instructions of the pregnancy test, wait three minutes and then read the results. If one pink line appears, that means, not pregnant. If two pink lines appear, it means that I was pregnant.
It took only thirty seconds for both pink lines to appear. It was instant like magic.

Oh my God. I'm pregnant! I'm going to have another child!
I have to call Emilio. He's going to be a father.
What have we done? Was it the right thing to do?
Can we afford another child? Will he be a good father?
Will I struggle the same as when I raised Bobby Jr. alone?
What about school?
A lot of unanswered questions ran through my mind.
I thought we had it all planned, but when the time came, it was excitedly overwhelming.

I called Emilio at work to tell him the news.
"You're going to be a father!"
I caught him off guard because he wasn't expecting the news so soon.

He was excited and his first words shocked me,
"Shudd up," at that time, we used that phrase a lot. It was one that he got from me.
It meant, stop playing and for real.
"Yup, I just took the pregnancy test and it came back positive."
He was scared but didn't want to show it. He may have thought the same things that ran through my mind.
He wanted me to confirm it with something more concrete than the home pregnancy test and questioned the accuracy of it. He wanted to make sure it wasn't a *false* reality. He couldn't believe I got pregnant so fast. I explained to him that it was one of the most accurate pregnancy tests on the market. I said that I will go to the clinic to get another pregnancy test to confirm it.
I went to the clinic to confirm it and showed him the results, and that's when it dawned on him that we were having a child.
His first child and my second one.
We were having a baby together.
Our Innocent One will arrive in nine months to add to our existing family.
We were happy and scared, but excited.

Chapter 25

My New Love

I kept Raphael in the loop with all my relationships. He knew that he and I could no longer hang together because Emilio and I were *serious and head over hills for each other*. Emilio loved me since our *first* conversation on AOL. It was love at first chat.

Raphael thought it was another run in the mill, and as soon as Bobby Sr. was released from prison that I would leave Emilio and run back to my husband. Raphael *thought* he knew me too well. He and I were both going to UTSA and we would often see each other at school and he'd always ask me,
"So, when does Bobby get out of prison?"
My response was the same each time, "I don't know and it has nothing to do with *my man and me.*"
"Ohhhhh, you are going to leave his ass as soon as Bobby is released from jail."
"Watch me," I'd emphasize with an annoyed repulse.
Raphael couldn't get over the fact that I left him when my husband was released, but in all honesty, my husband being released was only ONE reason I left, and truth be told, it wasn't meant for us to be together.
He was a good man but, he was not the man for me. Emilio was the man for me.

Before I met Emilio, I tried to hook Raphael up with a nurse that I worked with named, Kimberly. She often saw Raphael at my job so she knew how he looked and who I was referring to.
She wanted roses too, seeing that Raphael always brought me gifts.

I talked to Kimberly about Raphael and suggested that they hook up since they both were single. Kimberly was a good woman and she had a son that was a year or two younger than my son.

Raphael and Kimberly spoke on the phone a few times and I *think* they went out on a date.

Long story short, she said that she was no longer interested because Raphael talked about me too much.

A little after that incident is when Raphael met another woman from his home country in Nigeria.

I was happy for him, and he showed me pictures of him and her when he last visited Nigeria.

She was a beautiful African woman, and they made a great couple. Raphael was happy and so was I.

🎼 🎼 🎼

Emilio and I planned for our baby after the final confirmation of the pregnancy. Our lives were about to change and we were scared. We were bringing another child into the world.

I didn't know if it was for the good or bad, but every passing day, I had trepidations and wondered if it was the right thing to do.

I'd gone through so much with Bobby Sr. that I didn't want to relive any part of being a single mom. A single mother was the most difficult job in the world.

When I first went back to school and was raising my son, alone, I was afraid.

I had a fear of failure, but I didn't want to let my son down.

I wanted to give him the best life possible and I wasn't going to let fear deter me.

🎼 🎼 🎼

One day, before I returned to school at San Antonio College, I was at my sister, Terrie's house, and one of her friends was also in school and she was attending San Antonio College.

She was a few semesters ahead of me so she thought she knew everything.

She asked what English class I was going to take, and I told her, "Freshman Composition 1301."

I explained to her how I was returning to school after ten years.

"Oh no, you should start with a remedial English class instead of going straight into Freshman Composition. You will probably struggle since you've been out of school for so long," she insisted.

I asked what English course she was taking and she said, Freshman Composition 1301, but that she would be good since she already took a remedial English course last semester.

I suggested that we take the class together and she agreed. She thought that I wanted assistance from her and the reason that I suggested that we take the course together.

I didn't need her; I wanted to *prove* to her that I didn't need a remedial English course; even though, I hadn't been in school for ten years.

Her name is Charita and she was about 5'9" and weighed over 210lbs. She wore glasses and was built like the actor, Queen Latifah. She is darker than Latifah.

Charita was ghetto. Everything about her was ghetto.

Our first day of English class, she walked in late and sat next to me, but in a row over. She sat there comfortable and confident as Professor Kelly talked about her expectations to pass her course. I was nervous and anxious, but ready for whatever came my way.

The professor introduced herself and she had the students introduce themselves.

Shortly after the introductions, the professor passed out our first assignment.

I looked down at the assignment and the first question was,

"What is a noun?"

Oh yes, I know what a noun is. I wrote down my answer with confidence. Question number 2,

"What is a verb?"

This is not as bad as I thought. I know what a verb is and I'm feeling real confident that I made the correct decision not to take a remedial English course.

I got to question number 3,

"What is a preposition?"

Huh? What? Damn, I'm stumped. I can't remember what a preposition is. I panicked, but decided to go to the next question,

"What is an adverb?"

My confidence was back and I was rolling again. I remembered everything about adverbs.
The final questions on the assignment asked to correct the following sentences.
I answered all those questions with confidence, and when I finished with those questions, I returned to question number 3,
    "What is a preposition?"
I was lost. Dammit. I give up! I couldn't remember prepositions.

    After class, Charita and I talked, and she asked what I thought about the class assignment. I told her that I couldn't remember prepositions.
    She said, "Oh, a preposition is like, "on, in, under, over" and she continued to rattle off prepositions. She said, "To pretend like you have a house, a preposition are words that describe where an object can be placed within the house."
    I felt defeated that she knew *all* about prepositions, but I couldn't remember a thing about a preposition. Maybe I should have started with a remedial English course, my inner conscious tried to convince me.
Oh, hell no. I told my inner conscious, I must step my game up.

    Our next assignment, the professor wanted to see our writing skills. The assignment instructions was to tell her about ourselves.
Oh, that's easy, I thought to myself.
I got this one since I know everything about me.
I wrote my paper that night when I got home.
I talked about being a single mother, what my goals were, and how I was going to accomplish them.

𝄞 𝄞 𝄞

    The next class session, we turned in our assignments, and the following week our papers were graded and returned to us.
    The professor announced good and bad news to the class. She stated that she graded our papers and if you have a big red "X" across your paper then you need to see her after class. She was irritated because a lot of students had so many issues with their writing skills, and how some of the papers were written in "spoken language" and not "written language." She explained that writing in "spoken language" was a no-no in writing proper English.

She talked about another student in our class that was advanced in writing, but she was in a Master's program, and something happened that caused her to retake Freshman Composition. The professor said that she needed a dictionary when grading her paper because of her advanced vocabulary.

Professor, Kelly began passing back our graded papers, and you could clearly see the students with a big red "X" across their papers.
Pleaseeeeee, don't let me be one of those students with a big red "X," especially when Charita could see my paper. I already didn't know what a preposition was and I don't want a paper with a big red "X." Please, my confidence can't take another hit.
The professor started coming to the back towards the middle of the room where I sat and Charita sat right next to me in the next row over.
I sighed as my professor handed me my folded paper for discretion.
I began to open my paper and before I could open it, Charita leaned her body and face to see what I got on the assignment. I thought to myself, can you please give me the opportunity to see my own paper? Geeeezzzz...
I continued as if I didn't see or hear Charita. I looked at my paper and saw red, and my heart skipped more than two beats. I proceeded to look at my paper and processed the red marks, but it wasn't the big red "X" like I saw on other student's papers.
My red marks read,
"Not Bad At ALL. The writing will get more mature."
I saw the corrections she made in red ink and I was shocked at how little corrections there was on my paper.
I thought to myself, writing all those letters to Bobby Sr. in jail paid off and kept my writing skills afloat.

A little after I got my paper, the professor handed Charita her folded paper.
She opened her paper and that's when I saw it up close and personal, A big red "X" across Charita's paper.

Charita was red hot; she was livid, and if she wasn't of a darker hue, she would have turned the same color as that big red 'X" across her paper.
 I tried to calm her down and asked to see her paper in case the professor made a mistake.
I read the first paragraph of her paper and could barely get through the rest.
 Charita talked about how she sold drugs and her mother was in prison. She talked about shooting dice. It was a paper full of ghetto garbage written in spoken language.
 The professor explained to the class the difference between written and spoken language.
"Spoken language" is to be used when you are speaking to a friend. It is informal language and never used in an educational setting."
"Written language" is formal and is language that should be written on resumes and educational setting. I will not accept any papers that are not written in "written language."
 Charita's paper fit the description of 'spoken language' to the "T," like the "T" in my name. In other words, her writing was so jacked up that even autocorrect rejected it.
Her paper deserved two big red "X's," instead of one, and I think the professor did her a great service on that assignment by only giving her *one* red "X."

 The next class period, my professor said that the students that received a big red "X" on their papers need to go to the tutoring lab across the hallway.
 She explained that whenever she assigns a task, if we need help, then go to her office and leave our assignments in her cubby, and she would proofread and correct our papers before they are turned in for a grade.
 Why did my professor tell me this? I took every opportunity to get an "A" in the class, and every assignment we received, my paper was in my professor's cubby for proofreading.
Every assignment that she returned, I *earned* an "A."

My professor made an announcement to the class that many of us were not taking advantage of leaving our papers in her cubby for proofreading. The only student that's taking advantage of it is, TAMMY. She said that every time she checked her cubby, there was a paper from TAMMY.

She started to sing, the Michael Jordan's "Like Mike" song,
"Sometimes, I dreammmmm, that I am he,
"I wanna be like, Tammy!
I wanna be like, Tammy!"

I was embarrassed but elated while she took the time to shout-out my hard work and dedication to the entire class. Especially, so that Charita could hear it.

𝄞 𝄞 𝄞

The semester ends and I acquired an "A" in Freshman Composition 1301 and Charita earned a big fat,"C."

It was gratifying because if anyone that knows me, they know how competitive I am and knows not to ever tell me what I should and shouldn't do or what I can or can't do. How dare Charita tell me that I should take a remedial English course before taking Freshman Composition 1301?

Ha! How about you take two remedial courses before Freshman Composition and you would have acquired an "A" like me? How about that Ms. Smarty pants?
I bet on me every time because I will exceed all expectations.

𝄞 𝄞 𝄞

Professor, Kelly was my favorite teacher, and she taught me so much about writing proper English.
She was always open and willing to help her students if you took advantage of it. She and I became very close, and I continued to put my papers in her cubby from my Freshman Composition II course. She'd proofread *all* my papers.

She got married to a guy in the military and moved to another state shortly after the semester that I took Freshman Composition II.

I still think of her to this day. She was a huge inspiration, not only in an educational setting, but in my everyday life.

I went to Target and created a personal thank you card for her. I didn't have much money, but I wanted to get her something to show how much I appreciated her and what she meant to me.

I designed her card beautifully by a machine that Target had back in the days made specifically for creating sentimental hallmark type cards.

I made her the card and was prepared to give it to her until I looked at her cubby that displayed her full name, and I noticed that I spelled her new married last name wrong!

Oh noooooooooooo!
How could I give her this personally designed card, but her last name was spelled wrong?
She's an English professor. I can't give her this personalized card with a misspelling.

I was emotionally distraught and took the card and put it in my backpack and ran off before she saw me in her office space.

The semester ended, and technically, she hadn't been my professor since I first returned back to school. She was kind enough to continue proofreading my papers even though she was no longer my professor.

I didn't want her to see me and ask what I was doing in her office, so I blasted out of there.
I was so hurt that I wanted to cry.

She was leaving the state and I spelled her new last name wrong.
She will leave without knowing how much she meant to me. I took the card out of my backpack to look at how nice it was crafted and thought to myself that she'll never receive this card.
It was so beautiful and I know she would have loved it *if* her new married last name wouldn't have been misspelled.

Maybe, one day, my professor will read this book to know how much she meant to me. I hope so.

𝄞 𝄞 𝄞

I had fun at San Antonio College with my professors. I had another professor for my C++ programming class named, Mr. English. He would call out all the students that made a 100% on his written exams.

One day, he announced that there is only *one person* that made a 100% score.

The class waited and wanted to know who that **one** student was... I waited impatiently and thought to myself, I bet you, it's that girl from India.
If you know foreign students, you'll know that they come to America to live the American dream and are very dedicated and are some Brainiac's. She was *always* announced as one of the students that made 100% on the written exams, so I knew it was *her*.

"And the student that made the only 100 on the exam is, TAMMY!" Professor, English announced through his glasses that sat low on the top of his nose.

"OHHHH MYYYY GODDDDD, I CAN'T BELIEVE IT," I placed both my hands on each cheek of my face in disbelief.

The class erupted with laughter because of my acting theatrical skills that I demonstrated when *my* name was announced.

"Hell, I can't believe it, either," Professor English mumbled under his breath, but still loud enough for the class to hear.

The class laughed louder. Professor English was known for his profanity during class. He'd be teaching and shout out a curse word and never apologized for it.

He didn't give a damn. He figured, if you are in college then you are an adult, and if you aren't an adult, it's probably not the first nor the last time you'll hear profanity.

He and I would go back and forth with sarcasm in class and often made the class laugh.

One day, I was debugging my computer program and I had one error. I ask Mr. English if he could help me solve my error.

He was debugging my program and now I had seven errors.

"Mr. English, before you came over here to help me, I only had one error. Now, I got seven errors," I said

"Well, hell, I probably shouldn't help you then," he clapped back at me.

He reminded me of my computer math teacher, Mr. Hall at Fox Tech when I was a senior. He and I would go back and forth. He'd send me to the office a lot because of my sassy mouth. He said something to me one day, I can't recall what he said, but I told him, "That's mighty white of you." He cracked up laughing. I got that comment from George Jefferson. The Jefferson's was my favorite after school T.V. show.

Years later, I was doing the same thing to Professor, English. There are countless stories and fun that I had at San Antonio College.

🎼 🎼 🎼

By the time I met Emilio, I had already transferred to UTSA where I was finishing my final semesters to earn my Bachelor's degree in Information Systems.

Emilio and I only knew each other for eight months before we took the leap of faith to go half on a baby. Our relationship moved fast.

He attended my prenatal doctor visits and was anxious to learn the gender of the baby.

During our initial prenatal visit, a doctor that was referred to me by my friend, Evelyn examined my uterus and told me some discerning bad news during the doctor's visit.

The doctor said that he would like for me to return so that he could do a sonogram because I have a tilted uterus and the baby could be growing in my Fallopian tubes.

I was beyond terrified to hear him say that my baby could be in my tubes.

I walked in the visitors' waiting area to tell Emilio the bad news; we went home shaken, worried, and cried that our baby could be growing in my Fallopian tubes.

We cried and cried while trying to calm each other down.
It was one of the saddest days of our relationship.
We wanted the baby so bad.

Emilio called his aunt that worked at the University hospital to ask about Fallopian tube babies and what the doctor told me about my uterus.

His aunt was a saving grace for the time being because she said that I would be in pain if the embryo was in my tubes.

I was not in any pain physically but hearing that my baby could be in my Fallopian tube caused me heartache and pain.

Emilio and I went to the public library and researched Fallopian tubes and everything that had to do with childbirth complications.
Emilio being a religious man, didn't believe our baby was in my tubes. He declared that when we go for the sonogram, it will show that his baby was fine.

    We returned to the doctor's office a week later for the sonogram. Emilio was in the room with me.
I laid down on the table and raised my blouse so that the sonographer could spread the gel on my stomach. The gel was used to probe sound waves that reflect off the body.
The sonographer video recorded our baby; and as soon as the test was over, he gave us the recordings on VHS tape.
    We were nervous, but we had faith, and Emilio knew our baby was not in my tubes.
    We looked at the T.V. monitor of the sonogram and heard sound waves and saw the embryo inside my uterus and not my Fallopian tubes. We breathed a sigh of relief.
Our baby was doing fine chilling inside of her mommy.
It was the happiest day of our lives.

𝄞 𝄞 𝄞

    We went home with the good news and shared it with his mother. His family was relieved because they wanted a baby boy and they put a lot of emphasis on the gender of my unborn child. They wanted to continue the "Brooks" name to hand down from generation to generation.
    The Brooks family got on my last nerve with the gender of *my* unborn child.
I wanted a *healthy child.*
If the baby was a boy, I'll have two healthy boys.
If the baby was a girl, I'll have a boy and a girl; a little mini-me, so the gender never mattered to me.
    It wouldn't be until four months, we'd know the gender of our Innocent One.

Chapter 26

The End Is Near

🎼

Four months into my pregnancy and it was the moment the Brooks' family waited for. It was time to see the doctor and learn the gender of our unborn child.

I was excited but thought about not having the Ultrasound because of the emphasis put on the gender of my child, and it became very stressful. I never mentioned it to Emilio but I was tired of hearing about a 'boy' to carry on the Brooks' name. I didn't see anything *special* about the "Brooks" name. There was no great legacy tied to the name.

I don't think Emilio cared about the gender of his first-born child as much as *his* family. Emilio was a mama's boy when I met him. I didn't particularly like it and I needed to wean him off the breast milk.
He was thirty-one years old and even though he was a *man*, it was time to be a man and get from under the control of his family.

🎼 🎼 🎼

We arrived at the doctor's office. I reiterated to Emilio that I don't care about the gender as long as my child is healthy. Emilio wanted a boy only because of his family, but he'd be fine if it is a girl. The family put a lot of pressure on him and our baby's gender.

We were called into the doctor's office, I laid on the table like I'd done previously when the doctor said that our baby was in my Fallopian tubes. The sonographer spread the cold gel across my growing belly and the soundwaves of my unborn child could be heard along with the heartbeat. It was a rapid strong heartbeat. It was a blended thump, thumpy thump of mother and unborn child's heart.
I was excited to learn the gender of my child.

It looked as though the baby was asleep and we had to wake her or him to find out the gender.

The sonographer was like, "okay, turn around so we can see." He kept giving my stomach a little wiggle to turn the baby, and then we saw what we came to see.

The legs were open and we didn't see anything hanging and there it was…

The sonographer showed us that we were having a mini-me,
A GIRL!

I was so happy and thought about all the cute little dresses that I was going to buy her, but Emilio was indifferent.

Indifferent as though, I don't know if he was excited, scared, or disappointed because he didn't say much.

He was going to Natalia later that day to announce the news to his family that anxiously awaited a little boy.

We left the doctor's office in pursuit of our apartment.
I'd already had my baby names book on speed dial. I needed to know the sex of my child.

Emilio and I planned how we were going to buy a big bag of diapers each paycheck to make sure that our baby girl had everything she needed once she entered the world.

Her due date was December 26. The same birth date of her uncle, Jessie.

I wanted our daughter to be born before the end of the year so that I could claim her on my income taxes.

WE needed the extra money for our extended family.

𝄞 𝄞 𝄞

Emilio dropped me off at the apartment and drove to Natalia to deliver the news to his mother that he was going to have a baby girl.

He was still under his family's control, so he was a little disappointed to tell them that they were not going to have an extended grandson to carry on the 'Brooks' name; it was going to be a granddaughter that would carry the 'Brooks' name.

Emilio will never admit it, but he went down to Natalia to cry that he was going to have a girl and he was torn because of all the pressure put on him by his family.

I was excited about my little Mini-me and I didn't give a damn what the Brooks' family wanted.

I was going to be a proud mother of a little girlllllll! The Brooks' better get on board or else they will miss out on a beautiful grandbaby.

The Brooks family came to terms with the fact of having a little girl. Emilio and I said that we would try again for a boy, so it was no big deal.

During this time, Emilio promised to never hurt me, but he still beat the marriage drum even louder.
The pressure of marriage continued to enter our relationship and caused many disagreements.

He wanted to be married before his daughter was born. I was still married to Bobby Sr. and had no interest in marriage.
I was focused on naming my daughter, not marriage.

We asked Emilio's mother for a name for her granddaughter and she recommend the name, "Hannah."
We immediately disagreed on the name, Hannah. We were not naming our baby that white girl's name.
We didn't ask Mrs. Brooks for any more name recommendations after hearing, Hannah.

I want our daughter's name to have a purpose, a meaning, and most importantly, I want it to be unique. I want her to be the ONLY person in the world with the name.
I wanted her name to begin with the letter, "T" like my name.
I loved the way my mother named my sisters and me; Tina, Tammy, and Terrie so I continued with the letter "T."

I thumbed through the baby names book under the letter "T" when I saw the name,
"Tahira."
I thought to myself, that's a unique name and I have never heard of anyone named, "Tahira."
I looked up the meaning of the name, "Tahira" and it read, "Pure, Innocent, Virgin."
Hmmmmm, my baby girl will always be pure, innocent, and a virgin in my eyes.
I liked the name. The only thing that I didn't like was the spelling. It looked incomplete and I wanted to emphasize it more.

I got a sheet of notebook paper and wrote, "Tahira" on it.

I went to the Internet to see how many people were named, "Tahira." I saw a few people but not many. I thought, what if I add an "h" at the end of her name, and spelled it like, "Tahirah?"
That's it! That's it! I like it, I thought to myself. I wrote, Tahirah(pronounced Ta-hi-rah) Brooks on my notebook paper.

My daughter needs a middle name. I don't have a middle name and I've always wanted one, so my daughter *must* have a middle name.

Since the Brooks family wanted a boy to carry on their father "Jessie Brooks" legacy, I figured, I'll give her a name similar to his first name.
I couldn't name her "Jessie" because that was too common and masculine, and it wouldn't fit my little angel.

I opened the name book to look under the names that began with the letter "J."
I saw the name, Jasmine and thought, no, that's too common and not unique.
I continued reading and saw Jessica, but that was too white for me and still a common name.
I continued to read and that's when I saw, "Jessalyn"
OMG! That's it! It's similar to her grandfather's name and it's unique.
I took my notebook paper and wrote, "Tahirah Jessalyn Brooks"
What a name with a purpose.

I took my notebook paper that read, "Tahirah Jessalyn Brooks" written in print and cursive writing and I showed it to Emilio. He pronounced the first name wrong and I corrected him and he instantly liked the name.
I was elated that he liked it and our daughter's name was set in stone. *Tahirah Jessalyn Brooks.*

𝄞 𝄞 𝄞

Emilio was anxiously awaiting his daughter. He'd rub on my stomach and sing to the baby.
He'd buy me whatever I wanted to eat to make sure daughter and I were properly nourished.

All I did was eat. I ate so much that I changed doctors because he didn't allow pregnant women to gain more than two pounds per month during the entire pregnancy.

He was concerned with preeclampsia. Preeclampsia is common in pregnant women that caused high blood pressure and protein in the urine. Preeclampsia caused seizures in pregnant women and could be deadly. I didn't understand the seriousness of keeping my weight down since I have never had an issue with being overweight, especially during pregnancy with my son.

I continued to eat and the doctor didn't like it, so instead of stop eating, I changed doctors.

I searched for the doctor that delivered my son to see if he was still practicing, and he was.
I made the remainder of my prenatal appointments with Dr. Ricardo Munoz and I couldn't be happier because I didn't have to stop eating.

Emilio would buy me the Denny's breakfast special, three pancakes, eggs, and sausage before he and Bobby drove to Natalia each weekend.
He'd stop at my job in the morning with my breakfast.
When Bobby and Emilio returned to San Antonio, he'd stop at my job and bring me either tamales with Lay's potato chips or a Murph Burger with French fries.
I continued to eat and get fat, but thought I would lose the weight as soon as my daughter was born. I'd drop the weight immediately like I did when I had my son. So, I ate and ate.

September 11, 2001, I was seven months pregnant and I was at The University of Texas-San Antonio (UTSA) in the parking lot sitting in my car listening to the Tom Joyner Morning Show before my 9 a.m. class.

It was close to the time for my class to begin, so I got out my car and began to walk to class. I needed to make a stop at the computer lab so that I could print some homework papers.

I saw students standing at the front of the lab watching television. I didn't think anything of it but, it was more than the normal number of students standing and watching T.V. that caught my attention.

I wanted to see what they were watching and that's when I heard the news reporter talking about a plane crash in New York City. A terror attack that flew planes into the World Trade Center.

I didn't know anyone from New York, except for Walter. I think he was in Massachusetts at the time, so I continued watching the news.

I never heard of a terror attack with planes, and I thought, wouldn't the attackers have to kill themselves or maybe they jumped out of the planes with a parachute?
I heard the news reporters say, suicide bombers.
Suicide bombers? Who would kill themselves in that manner by flying a plane into a building causing it to explode?
Who would do that?

I had to go to class so I couldn't wait around to hear the answers to my questions.

I got to my first class and we talked about what happened in New York City. We didn't do much work in class. My professor released us early so that we could check on family and friends.

I didn't have any family or friends in New York, but I couldn't help but think about my unborn daughter that was growing inside my stomach.
My baby was due in a few months.
What kind of world would I bring my daughter into?
What have I done to bring my innocent baby into this cruel, crazy, messed up world?
I rubbed my stomach and held it tight.
I was terrified for humanity, but not only for humanity, I was terrified for my unborn baby girl.

I was scared like the time when I was a single mother; it was only Bobby Jr and me, and I'd wake up in the wee hours of the morning tired and sleepy from working two jobs, going to school full-time while taking care of my son alone.

I would get home from work; I'd set my alarm clock to 3a.m. so that I could get up and study for my school exams. I'd get home at midnight, get three hours of sleep and then get up to study for my exam. I'd ease out of bed so that I wouldn't wake my son.
I would turn the kitchen light on and sit at the kitchen table and I would cry my eyes out.

I didn't want to study. My eyes, feet, and brain were tired. I just got home from working double shifts on my feet all day, and I wanted to sleep, not study.
I'd sit there crying and feeling sorry for myself.
I had many fights with my subconscious. My subconscious would say,

"Nobody told you to have a baby with that sorry ass nigga. You should have stayed in school when you didn't have a kid. You were the one that chose this life. You are not a victim. You better get your ass up and study for this exam. Get your act together and study! Stop all that damn crying."

I would hate and love my subconscious. I loved the tough love it gave me but hated hearing the truth.
I was not a victim and after my mini breakdown and tears dropping all over my school work. I'd dry my tears and say, "You can do it, Tammy. Keep going. It will be better for you and your son."

It was better when I met Emilio, but now these terror attacks were scary and brought so much uncertainty.

The president, George W. Bush declared war on Afghanistan for the terror attacks against the United States of America, and our country was *temporarily* united.

Chapter 27

The Blue Ultimatum

T he further along I became in my pregnancy, it seemed like the more stress I encountered.
I had my man by my side and a few semesters left before I graduated from UTSA.

Emilio was busy listening to everyone around him about how and what he should do with *his* life.

He was an ordained minister of his church in Natalia. He'd been a church member since he was eighteen years old.

He respected his pastor, Mr. Green since he was the pastor that ordained him in 2001.
Emilio being ordained was a big deal, not only for him, but for his mother as well.

He was also in cahoots with what was *biblically* right and who he loved (me). A pregnant unmarried me.
He loved me and wanted to be married. I didn't want a child out of wedlock, but I didn't want to be pressured into marriage. I wanted it on my own time and accord.

Emilio was struggling with his faith, religion, and my *big* belly. He wanted marriage, but I was stubborn and wanted no part of it, and we clashed. I wanted a divorce from Bobby Sr. but I was not ready to jump into marriage, again. I was happy grinning and sinning, pregnant and married to Bobby Sr. not my current man, Emilio.

I contacted Legal Aid for one last time to see if they would grant me my divorce.

"Tammy, today is your lucky day. You have called each year for a divorce and have been told "no," since you have called almost every year, today we are going to grant you a divorce and an attorney will contact you. The attorney is free and if it's not a complicated divorce, your divorce will be finalized within three months," The representative of legal Aid said on the phone.

I couldn't believe my ears. Legal Aid was finally going to represent me and give me a FREE divorce.
I was excited and I told Emilio the good news.
Emilio was happy about the divorce and thought that we should be married soon after the divorce was final.

What? Huh? Marry *immediately* after my divorce? Wait a minute. Hold on.
I didn't want to get married *immediately* after my divorce.
I wanted to enjoy my freedom before getting married *again.*
I hadn't been single since I was a teenager. I'd finally be single, even though, I wouldn't be single, single because I have a man, but I wanted to enjoy l*egally* being single.

I loved Emilio and we were going to get married and be a family, but I was not ready for marriage, yet. I'm the type of person that I can't be rushed or pressured, if so, then I'd go into reserve mode. I had to go at my own pace or I would shut down.

Emilio knew my hang-up about being married. I knew his position on wanting to be married, and it caused a HUGE rip in our relationship.

It was so bad that Emilio gave me an ultimatum; his ultimatum was to get married after my divorce was final or else he was leaving. He wanted marriage and I was not having it.

I was caught up in my ego of "You don't tell me what I'm going to do." And I told him that there is the door and he could leave.

I was not going to be pressured into marriage.
I didn't want to be married, *yet.*

Emilio did exactly what I told him to do. He left and went home to Natalia.
I was nine months pregnant and now my daughter's father was gone.

My son was devastated. He loved Emilio and didn't want him to go.

It was many times when Emilio and I would have an argument and he stayed because of the love for Bobby Jr.

One time, we argued and I told Emilio to leave and before he could go, my son went into the bathroom and got some Vaseline and a plastic bag and put the plastic bag on the doorknob with the Vaseline on top. He didn't want Emilio to leave or go anywhere. He felt that if he put Vaseline all over the doorknob that Emilio wouldn't be able to open the door forcing him to stay.

When Emilio walked to the door to leave, he saw the plastic bag with the Vaseline on the doorknob and then looked at me; we looked at each other and the argument seized.

There was no way his heart would let him walk out the door that night. He stayed and there were many times that Emilio wanted to leave but stayed mainly because of the love for my son. I drove Emilio crazy. I don't see how he stayed and kept coming back.
He loved me, but he couldn't handle me.
I was damaged goods that fought demons of my past. He couldn't understand me, and in all honesty, I didn't understand me.
My hormones were tough to deal with, too.
My past was tough to deal with, and at times, I didn't blame Emilio if he wanted to leave. I would have left, too.

This time he left. He wanted marriage and if I wasn't going to give it to him, then there was no need to continue the relationship.

It was a few days since Emilio left. I was miserable without *my* man.
My son missed him, too. He wanted him back and would sneak on the phone and call Emilio without me knowing. He needed to hear his voice.

I wanted my man back home, but I wasn't going to adhere to his damn ultimatum. I wasn't going to change my position on marriage. How dare he give *me* an ultimatum? Humph. I'll get married when I want to. I promised him marriage *after* the baby and he agreed but now, he changed his mind. He wanted marriage *before* the baby.
He didn't want our baby coming into this world and not being married.

I wrote Emilio an email about my doctor's appointment. I told him about his daughter.

He responded to my email. He also sent me a poem that he wrote for his daughter.

Emilio and I started communicating again through email and then the phone.

He missed us and he was ready to come back home. His nephew messed up his SUV by putting diesel fuel in the gas tank so he didn't have transportation.

I told him that I would come to Natalia to pick him up.

It had been almost two weeks since he left.

I couldn't get to Natalia fast enough. I missed him so much.

We walked into the house and his mother, nephew, and sister were there.

We ate KFC, and soon after eating, Emilio was ready to go.

He didn't want me to talk to his mother, because I could get long winded and talk for hours. He was ready to go *home*.

His sister, Delaine said, "Ooohhhh, I know what y'all about to do."

She embarrassed me because she was right.

We had to make up for lost time.

I didn't know why he was in such a hurry to leave, but I didn't ask, I obliged and I left traveling back to San Antonio, Texas with *my man*, my son, and our unborn daughter, Tahirah.

Chapter 28

She Got My Nose

🎼

Emilio and I were back together and there was nothing or no one tearing us apart.
He finally stopped talking about marriage and we planned for our daughter. He pulled the ultimatum card, but it didn't work, so he decided to wait until I was ready.

    I met with the attorney from Legal Aid to get my divorce finalized.
    I signed papers stating that Bobby Sr. was not the father of my unborn daughter. He had been incarcerated for three years, how could he be the father of my unborn daughter? But according to Texas law, since I was legally married to Bobby Sr., my daughter was legally recognized as his child unless the proper paperwork was filed denying paternity.

🎼 🎼 🎼

    I became obsessed with delivering a healthy child for Emilio, and I wanted to have his baby bad, not only for me but most importantly for him. I purchased an over the counter baby heart monitor so that I could monitor my daughter's heartbeat and make sure that she was fine.
    I heard so many stillborn birth horror stories that I didn't want to take chances on my daughter being stillborn. I'd read that if you drink orange juice the fetus would become very active. So, when Tahirah wasn't moving around in my stomach for long periods of time, I'd shake my stomach, and if she still wouldn't move, I'd go to the refrigerator and drink orange juice. The orange juice trick worked each time.

    During final exams at school, I'd wake up at 3 a.m. or 4 a.m. to study for an exam and I'd wake Tahirah. The feeling of my daughter moving around inside me relieved a lot of stress, even if, it irritated her. I knew that she didn't get much sleep during my pregnancy because I was always checking on her by shaking my belly or drinking orange juice.

I would talk to her and tell her that she was in college and that WE had to study and that it wouldn't be long before WE graduated.
I dreamed of carrying Tahirah across the stage with me because she put in the early mornings and hours of studying, and she should be rewarded, too.

𝄞 𝄞 𝄞

There were many false labors going on towards the end of my pregnancy. I drove Emilio insane. Lordy, why he wanted to marry me was between him and God. Bless his heart.

One day, I told Emilio that I couldn't feel the baby move and the orange juice wasn't working, so he and I drove to the Nix hospital to have the doctors check me and sure enough, everything was fine.

It was December 27 and I wanted my labor induced. I was trying to have Tahirah before the end of the year to claim her on my taxes, but most importantly, I didn't want a stillborn child.
The doctor declined to induce my labor and sent me home.

Emilio, Bobby Jr, and I was in Natalia celebrating New Year's Day with the Brooks' family. I was taking pictures with Emilio's dad as he kissed my stomach with his first granddaughter inside.
Emilio's sister Delaine made tamales for me because she knew how much I loved them.
I had three dozen of tamales that I was taking back home. I had no symptoms of labor pain the entire day in Natalia.

𝄞 𝄞 𝄞

We get home around 5 p.m. and still no labor pains.
We were watching TV and I was lying in bed when I asked Emilio to warm me some tamales because I was hungry.
I ate about two jalapeno tamales and that's when I felt a slight pain in my stomach.
I told Emilio what I felt, but of course, he thought it was another *false labor*.

I told him that this one is *for real* and that we should call the doctor and head to the hospital.

Emilio contacted Dr. Ricardo Munoz and explained the pain that I had in my stomach.

Dr. Munoz asked how many minutes apart the pains were. After conversing with Dr. Munoz, it was time to go to the hospital. I had my suitcase packed with Tahirah and my clothes already prepared for the moment I was in labor.

𝄞 𝄞 𝄞

We made a stop at my sister, Tina's house so that should could take care of Bobby Jr and then we headed downtown to the Nix hospital.

The night was cold and there were ice flurries in the air dropping on the windshield of my 1993 white Ford Escort.
Emilio and I talked about how nice it was and that this was it, we were finally going to see our baby girl.
We were anxious and nervous all at the same time.

𝄞 𝄞 𝄞

I was admitted into the hospital by a nurse named, Tammy.
She had Emilio fill out all the paperwork and he could barely do it because he was so nervous.
She sensed his anxiety and made reference to it.

One of the questions was if this was my first pregnancy and Emilio thought that she was talking about him.
WE laughed because Emilio wasn't thinking straight. I don't know if it was him or me in labor watching him filled with anxiety.

He kept going to the restroom. His anxiety level was a ten.

𝄞 𝄞 𝄞

I didn't sleep that night, because of the labor pains.
They were getting stronger and stronger.
The nurses were coming in to check how many centimeters my cervix was dilated, but it still wasn't time to have our daughter.

Dr. Munoz came in around 3 p.m. in the afternoon the next day on to break my amino fluid sac.
Emilio's mother and brother arrived at the hospital a short time later.

I was in so much pain, but I was not given any pain medication, instead, the nurse gave me a shot inside my cervix so that it would *ease* the pain.

It didn't ease the pain, instead, it had me talking incoherently so that my mind could *think* that I wasn't in pain.
Whatever they were injecting in my cervix to make me think I was not in pain, made me say some of the dumbest things. Emilio laughed.

I thought of an actor in the movie, "Higher Learning" and wondered why he cut all his hair.

"I don't know why Remy cut off all his hair. Hmm, hmm, hmm," I said shaking my head side to side.

I thought in my mind that these nurses were trying to kill me and my baby, and I wanted Emilio to get me out of there.

One of the nurses told me that I would have an urge to push, but for me not to push, and that I had to hold it like if I wanted to take a shit but couldn't.

I laid there through hours of wanting to push, but fighting the urge not to push.

Emilio's mother sat there hopelessly and watched me fight through it all.
I thought that my baby and I were not going to make it.
I was tired, thirsty, hungry, and exhausted.
I prayed to God for strength to help me pull through.
I was giving up, but kept fighting for *my* baby.
I heard other women screaming and having their babies, but me, I laid there with the urge to push but couldn't push according to the nurse's orders.
It was almost 24 hours of labor and still no baby.

It was a little before 7p.m., when the nurse, Tammy, who admitted me into the hospital the previous day returned to work and walked into the room and said,
"You still haven't had your baby?"
She immediately checked my cervix to see how many centimeters I dilated and then she said, "it's time." She goes to the nurse's station to get a doctor.

It was a female doctor that I didn't recognize that came into my room to check my dilated cervix.

The nurses assisted her in getting me prepared to bring my baby girl into the world.
     Emilio sat in a chair on my left side of the bed, holding my hand, but kept his head turned the entire time that I was told to PUSHHHHHHH!
I bit my tongue and made the ugliest face, and I did what I was told, and I PUSHHHHHHHEDDD!
     The doctor said that Tahirah was big and that she would have to cut my vagina, and after the episiotomy, I PUSHHHHHEDD one last time and that's when the pain ends and my daughter slid out of my vagina like a glowing little naked shiny angel.
     "She got my nose!" Emilio's first response when he saw Tahirah. I laid there anxiously waiting to hold and see what my baby girl looked like. She had a head full of black wavy and straight hair.
She wasn't wrinkled, bloody, or full of feces matter like I envisioned or how most babies are when they are born.
She was amazingly perfect.
I'm not saying it because she is my daughter, but it was how she was born.
The doctor laid Tahirah on my chest, and she was heavy to my fragile body. I had no strength to hold my beyond perfect, daughter.
I was exhausted and relieved that it was all over and that we both made it.
     Everyone in the room glowed over Tahirah and I was forgotten about for the time being, but I didn't mind, my Angel Cakes had arrived.

     It was a miracle that she and I made it because the nurses at Nix hospital were either incompetent or prejudice because they almost killed my daughter and me.
     Emilio's mother told me years later that one of the nurses was playing with Tahirah's hair twirling it around her finger while she was in my vagina. I couldn't believe it.
     The nurse, Tammy saved our lives, because I was ready to deliver hours ago when I was told not to push. The nurse lied about my cervix not being dilated to ten centimeters. I held on and knew they were trying to kill me and I wanted to walk out the hospital.
     My Mighty Creator of the earth said, "Not today" and he lifted my Innocent One and me above it all. We made it! We were resilient.

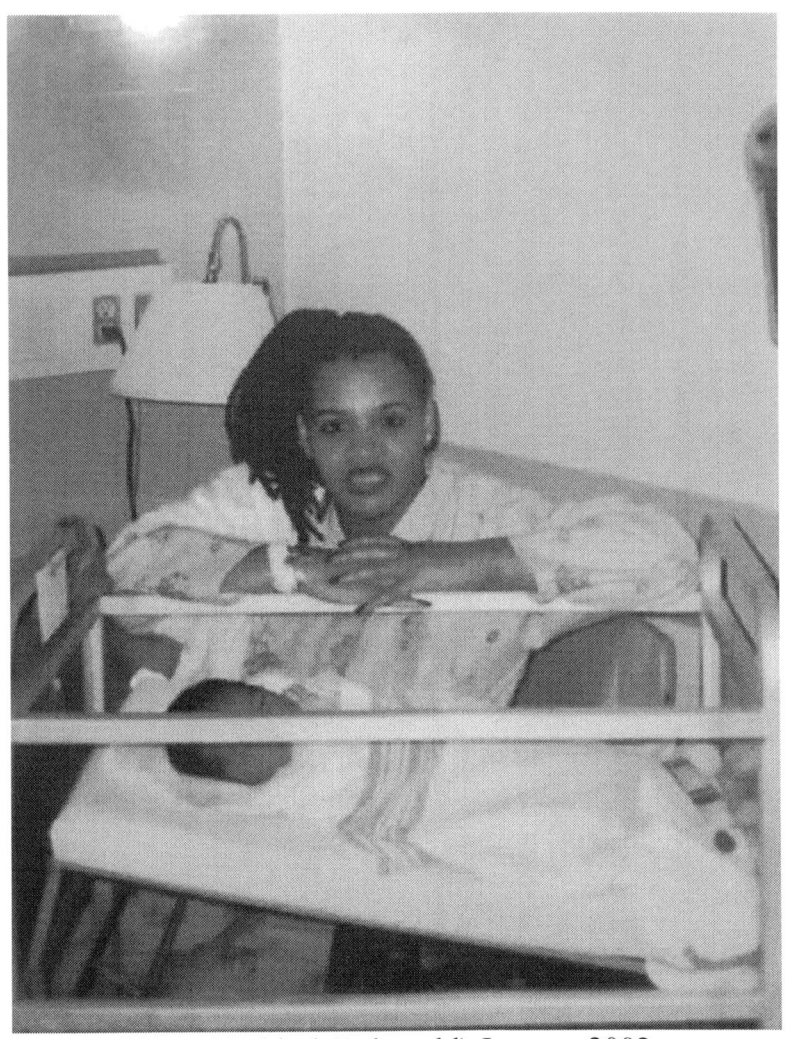
Tammy(32) and Tahirah(1 day old) January 2002.

Chapter 29

Bells Will Be Ringing

Our daughter arrived in January 2002 and my divorce from Bobby Sr. was final in March 2002.

Emilio and I went to the courthouse within that week to purchase our marriage license to be married. He had been good about not pressuring me, so I was *finally* ready for marriage. We had our baby girl and we didn't want to waste any more time. I promised that I would marry him *after* the baby.
I had my divorce decree and we were ready to become husband and wife.

The courthouse representative read my divorce decree and noticed that it was recently finalized.
She informed Emilio and me that we had to wait at least ninety days to purchase our marriage license because my divorce was just finalized.

Our daughter was two months old and we didn't want to wait another minute to be married. We were disappointed but planned to return to the courthouse soon after the ninety days waiting period ended.

For some reason, Emilio and I didn't return to the courthouse after the ninety days, it wasn't until my last semester of college that I announced to Emilio that he and I will marry before I walked across the stage. Emilio was ecstatic and so was I.

We purchased our marriage license and set the date of May 02, 2003 to become husband and wife. The wedding date was a week before my graduation.

May 02, is also the anniversary date of his oldest brother. I had no idea his brother was married on the same date, otherwise, I probably would have rescheduled.

Emilio kept it a secret of his brother's anniversary date because he was ready to be married and he wasn't going to let anything get in the way of me becoming his wife.

Emilio and I notified both families of our plans to marry and we set everything within a week.
I went to the mall and purchased my dress. Emilio got his attire together and we are ready to be married. I had a lot of things going through my head because I was graduating within a week. My daughter was one year's old and she was spoiled rotten. She wanted to be carried by either daddy, mama, brother, or her grandmother and that was it.
She started walking at nine months old so she was running by the time Emilio and I were set to be married.

On our wedding day, Emilio was running around like a chicken with no head. He was in Natalia trying to get the reception barbeque food ready for after our wedding ceremony, which was scheduled to take place downtown at the courthouse.
We didn't have a pot to pee in between the two of us, but we had each other and most importantly, we had *endless love*. We made a promise to one another that we were going to build together and our finances were going to get better.

My sisters, brother, and nieces attended the wedding ceremony on my side of the family and Emilio's mother was there at the courthouse, while his brother Jessie stayed behind to barbeque and prepare the food for after we said our vows. Emilio's friend, Manny was his 'best man.'

I arrived at the courthouse with my family before Emilio, and I was a little worried about Emilio arriving. I had crazy thoughts going through my head of him leaving me at the altar, even though, I knew he loved me and desired to get married a long time ago.

As we walked down the street to the courthouse, I saw Emilio and his mother driving down the street looking for parking so that he could meet *me* at the altar.
We were getting married. It was finally happening. I was there and so was my man to say, "I dooooooooooo."

Bobby Jr. was ten years old and he gave me away to Emilio. Soon after the wedding ceremony ends, Bobby Jr. no longer called, Emilio by his nickname, Nino. He called him, *dad*, and he has been his dad from May 02, 2003 until now. He never called him anything else, other than, *dad*.

After the ceremony, my family and I drove to Natalia, Texas for our reception that was held at his brother's Jessie house. He had a huge backyard and it was perfect for what we needed.

The Campbell family was the only family dancing to the music. The Brooks' were not dancers, instead, they watched us get down, my brother, sisters, nieces, and nephew. We were line dancing and thought we were back at Prime-Time nightclub in our younger days.

I had to convince my *husband* to dance with me because he was too shy to dance in front of everyone.

We all had a good time at our wedding that cost maybe $250.00 total.

After the reception, Bobby, Tahirah, and my niece, Argentina along with my other family members drove back to San Antonio, Texas. I had to work the next morning so I wanted to get home before midnight.

My husband and his friend, Manny stayed a little longer and were expected to return home later.

It was maybe an hour of returning home, I received a phone call from my mother-in-law telling me that my *husband* had too many beers to drink and drive, and she didn't want him to drive home.
I heard his sister, Sandra's voice in the background trying to calm him down.
He didn't want to stay in Natalia and wait until he sobered up, he wanted to come home.

"Leave me alone! I want to go home to my wife!" I heard my husband say in the background. He kept repeating over and over, that he wanted to go home to his WIFE.

His mother handed him the phone to see if I could calm him down.

I talked to my *husband* and asked him to calm down and assured him that I was not going anywhere. I wanted him to be safe and to please drink the V8 tomato juice so that he could sober up and then come home to his wiffffeeeee. He said that he wasn't drunk. He is a social drinker so I was surprised when they told me he was drunk. His mom blew everything out of proportion.

My husband reluctantly obliged and calmed down. I don't think he waited for an hour because he was home a little after an hour. I was happy that my husband was safe at home in my arms.

Emilio(33) Tammy(33) May 2003 Wedding Day

The next day, my husband received a phone call from his mother informing him that the night of our wedding, that someone stole her seven hundred dollars out of her purse. It was her bill money.

I was distraught and hurt. I called my family to ask if they saw anyone spending money because someone stole my mother-in-law bill money. They all said that they were not in the room where her purse was located.

My family was outside dancing the entire time, so I know it wasn't the Campbell family that stole her money. It was probably Emilio's brother's wife side of the family. They knew the layout of the house and where the purse was located.

The thief of my mother-in-law's money ruined my husband and my perfect wedding day. I cried, I was so upset.

I don't know who took the money to this day but I'm sure they will pay the price for what they did.

May 06, 2003, I walked across the UTSA auditorium to acquire my Bachelors of Business Administration in Information Systems degree. Pee Tee and Bobbie Jean's daughter did it! All my hard work, tears, and late nights paid off. I did it, mama and daddy! I graduated in the ***Top 15% of the College of Business graduates in 2003***.

Tammy(33)
UTSA Graduation Day May 2003.

Edward(35) ,Tina(37), Terrie(31), Tammy(33).UTSA Graduation.

Ryans Steakhouse
Celebrating Tammy's graduation. (2003)
Emilio, Tammy, Tahirah, Terrie, Tina, Edward, (brother's girlfriend).
Bobby Jr, Carl, Argentina, Carla, Meoshia, June(Tina's boyfriend).

On August 26, 2006, my husband and I closed on our first home. It is a two story 2600 square foot, 3 bedrooms, 2 ½ baths, 2 car garage home. It's not perfect, but it's a start.

We put in motion what we said we were going to do when we first got married. We promised that we were going to build together and we have.

Our journey is not easy and neither is it over. We still have more to go. We overcame a lot of challenges within our relationship.
We are still together and continue to live a simple life in our first home. Our kids are healthy and doing well.

Bobby Jr. has always had an entrepreneurial skill set in him. When he was a little boy, he did things to make money; such as, selling his new and used toys that he no longer wanted. He would go door to door selling his toys to the neighbors.

He choreographed dance routines for my husband and me to watch by putting on talent shows. We had to *pay* a nickel to attend his talent shows. It was worth every nickel.

He has his own clothing line and you can visit his website at stateofvision.com

Tahirah was accepted into an early college school at the age of fourteen. There could only be 135 students chosen out of 3,500 eight-graders from five different Junior high schools, and she was one of the students that was accepted. She will graduate with an Associate's degree before she receives her high school diploma. She is self-motivated and learned to read when she was three years old.

Many people say that she's intelligent because I was pregnant with her when I was in school, but I disagree, she is intelligent because she works hard; and like my characteristics, Tahirah does not accept failure. She has been an honor roll student throughout school and plans to be a physician.

As far as, Emilio and I, we are going to retire in the world of peace, harmony, and less hostility. We plan to ride into the sunset together hand and hand. I will reminisce about the good and bad of surviving a life filled with blues, but also the happiness of Rhythm & Blues music that got me through it all, **The Ghetto Blues**.

Emilio told me when we first met that if he knew I was coming, he wouldn't have been with any other woman, he would have waited for me. He has always had a way with words, I will never forget him saying, "Tammy, if you were to die in 99 days, I'd want to die in 98 days because I wouldn't want to live one day without you."

Emilio(32) Tammy(32) Tahirah(5 months) Bobby(10) Year 2002.

Tahirah(2) Tammy(34) Emilio(34) Bobby(12) May 2004.

Emilio (39) Tammy(39) Bobby(16) Tahirah(7)

Bobby(24) Tammy(47) Tahirah(14) Emilio(47) November 2016. Dallas Cowboys vs Washington Redskins @ AT&T Stadium in Dallas TX.

Family Photos

Niece, Argentina, Niece, Meoshia, and sister, Terrie.

Tina, Tammy and, Thelma. (1996). Def Comedy Jam

Terrie(22), Tina(29), Tammy(25) (1994)
The country.

Graduation day 1987
Brother's girlfriend, Freddie Mae, Edward(19), Carl, Tina(21).

4 Generations of Women:
Great grandmother, Sammie Lee Hughes
Grandmother, Emma Jane Cline
Mother, Barbara Jean Campbell
Sisters, Tina, Tammy, and Terrie

Made in the USA
Middletown, DE
21 November 2018